# PRINCIPLES OF
# BICYCLE RETAILING III

## Other books by Randy W. Kirk

*Principles of Bicycle Retailing (1st and 2nd Editions)*

*Bicycle Retailers Guide to Getting Rich in the Recession*

*When Friday Isn't Payday*

# PRINCIPLES OF BICYCLE RETAILING III

## ALL NEW STRATEGIES FOR THE '90S AND BEYOND

### BY RANDY W. KIRK

*Third Edition, Revised and Expanded*

San Clemente, CA

## DEDICATION

To my "partner" Terry Brown, the only constant in my life over the past twelve years. Thank you for all your words of encouragement.

## ACKNOWLEDGMENTS

A special thank you to Grace Rachow for her slashing red pen, without which much of the material here-in would be far less readable. Thanks also to AC International public relations director Greg Harrison for his editorial review.

Thanks also to Herb Wetenkamp for all his support over the years in bringing my ideas into the marketplace.

Cartoons by Rix Fernandez.
Cover by Kurt Smith.
Interior Design by Cindee Ross.

Info Net Publishing,
P.O. Box 3789, San Clemente, CA 92674
(714) 489-9292

*Printed in the United States of America*

ISBN 0 924272 05 8

# PREFACE

The changes that have taken place in retail bicycle shops during the past ten years have been substantial as well as dramatic. In the early eighties it was the rare store that offered any self-service. Specialty cycling clothes were offered only in the "tech" shops. Computerization was not a consideration. Fax machines were called facsimile machines and were only used by major corporations.

The front window was just a place to line up more bicycles. It wasn't considered dignified to "sell" bicycles. The only advertising was in the Yellow Pages. Margins on bicycles rarely topped 30%, and most owners didn't realize that freight and assembly were part of cost in determining profit margin.

Catalog sellers were a nuisance, but not the major factor they represent today. There were twice as many distributors, but only four of these were national in scope. It was possible for a retailer to make a living at $125,000 in annual sales. There were only two or three shops in the country doing over $1,000,000, and none were approaching $2,000,000.

There was only one major consumer magazine devoted to cycling, and local tabloids were amateurish efforts produced by local clubs on typewriters. Most shops were started or owned by folks who liked to repair bicycles.  Nobody had ever heard of slatwall.  In-store merchandising usually consisted of putting some close-outs in a wire basket with a hand-written cardboard sign.

What a difference a decade makes!  Let's take a look into the future, and imagine how bicycle retailing will be done in the year 2000.

It doesn't make me happy to start out with an unfortunate, but inescapable reality—the "Mom and Pop" bicycle shop will go the way of "Mom and Pop" ice cream parlors and drug stores.  In all but the smallest and most rural communities, bicycle retail outlets will be serious business enterprises.  Most will be either megastores or multiple-outlet chains owned and staffed by trained professionals.

The service department will shrink even further in importance as bicycles become increasingly trouble and maintenance free, and as labor costs become totally prohibitive.  Lost service revenue will be made up by additional sales of accessories, clothing, and upgrades.  The efficiency of better management will lead to increased margins.

Interior design will continue to improve to the point where even smaller shops will more closely resemble slick clothing boutiques.  Retailers will find they can realize higher sales and profits from learning about store layout, interior lighting, and product presentation than from repairing a broken spoke.

Every store will have computers.  Products will be bar-coded.  Orders will be placed with major vendors by direct computer link up (called EDI, Electronic Data Interface).  Even consumers will be communicating with retail outlets by computer and fax as product and price lists become electronic. Owners of single outlets and small chains may find they need to co-operate with other lower volume bicycle sellers in order to compete with the chain stores' purchasing power.

Consumer magazines and tabloids will lose influence to electronic media. Articles, product information, and advertising will be available on the television screen through cable networks, phone company services, and electronic magazines.

The industry will become even more international in scope. Buyers will be offered an amazing array of choices as numerous emerging democracies and third-world countries play a fast game of catch-up with the industrialized West and Pacific Rim. Don't be surprised to see rubber from India, electronics from Viet Nam, and built-up bicycles from Argentina.

The USA will experience more dramatic changes in population alignments (demographics). There will be lots and lots of seniors. Thirty-something will no longer be the "in" age, because the population of people between the ages of twenty and forty will be insignificant compared to the number of aging baby boomers, and under- twenty echo-boomers.

Before the end of the century, the U.S. will be starved for entry-level employees. It is likely that the current efforts to limit illegal immigration or importation of inexpensive manufactured goods will be replaced by efforts to increase immigration and imports.

There will be many changes over the next several years. Some of these changes will represent opportunities for those who are quick to respond to change and challenge. Others will fail to see the change or refuse to adapt. They will undoubtedly lose their businesses.

Even with all the changes we will see in the coming decade, there are some important elements of business practice which are timeless. Customer service, employee management, sales professionalism, cash flow management, personal desire, commitment, development and maintenance of vendor relationships, and ethical business practices will still lead the list of elements of business success into the 21st Century.

In the pages that follow, every element of the successful bicycle retail enterprise will be explored. The information, concepts, and ideas are all specific to the two-wheel, human powered industry where I have spent my entire career. I hope that you will find this book to be a reference tool that will not only stimulate you to take certain actions immediately, but will also be kept close at hand as a reference source to be read again and again.

— *Randy Kirk*

# TABLE OF CONTENTS

Smith
&
Smith
Bankruptcy Law

Out of
Business

Prepare Yourself For Failure.

# CHAPTER 1

# SEVEN REASONS WHY BICYCLE SHOPS SUCCEED

Traditional "how to run a business" literature always contains a list of the reasons why the enterprises under discussion fail. It seems to me that more benefit might be derived from examining those winning features which consistently appear in successful bicycle shops. The first and most important reason for success in any enterprise is

## Reason #1 - Your Heart's DESIRE

You have to want it, and want it **bad**! Your desire to be successful is going to mean giving up some things you may also have a strong desire to do... things like sleeping, eating normal food at normal times, relaxing, socializing, and bicycling. You can pretty well count on spending less time with your spouse, kids, and friends, to say nothing of your television.

Then there is the issue of family finances. While you are in the process of becoming successful, your spouse and children should be ready to scale back and work from a budget (good advice for everyone, but essential during the growth stage of a small business).

Is it possible to lead a normal life and run a bicycle shop at the same time? There are probably examples of people who have opened their doors with plenty of capital, evaluated the market in every detail, started in a perfect retail climate, and were the beneficiary of every lucky break along the way. It's possible that one such as that might work only 40 hours, still buy a new car every three years, and keep up on how the hometown team is doing.

For the rest of us less fortunates, anything short of a maximum effort in time, energy, and emotional commitment is going to leave us with less than a fighting chance.

Here are other tell-tale signs that indicate you have enough desire to make your business into a great asset:

1. When crisis rears its ugly head, you don't get worried . . . you get busy.

2. Slow days are times for planning, cleaning, and developing ideas for getting more people in the door, not moping, watching soap operas and game shows, or staring blankly out of the soot-covered windows.

3. The visits of sales representatives are occasions for learning, negotiating, and making well-considered decisions, not grumbling about how tough business is.

4. Every unoccupied moment is spent reading trade magazines, consumer bicycle magazines, and other books and periodicals that will expand your knowledge and ability.

5. Every day is seen as an opportunity for improvement.

6. Failures are acknowledged as important building blocks to success.

Will there come a day when you will be able to work 40 or even fewer hours per week, not take home the shop problems, and begin to replace the wieners and beans with an occasional T-bone? Sure. Many dealers are already there . . . and then some. However, for the rest, the harder you work now, the sooner you'll reach the brass ring. You should expect to put in at least five to ten years of hard work to reach a level where you can start to breathe easy.

That five to ten years may be the first years of business. They may come later, when you realize you are in trouble. You may put in two hard years in the beginning, relax, get in trouble, and then put in the other eight. But unless your circumstances are very special, you will have to put in the years of hard work in order to establish a thriving business.

2

## Reason #2 - You Learn How to SELL

The general title of one who owns a retail establishment is still "merchant." A merchant is someone who sells things. If you are not a skilled sales person, it will be very difficult for you to hire, train, and motivate salesmen.

Nothing happens in any business until something is sold. You can have a great location, superb computerized bookkeeping capability, incredible advertising, and the most beautiful exterior and interior ever created. If, however, the people come flocking to your enterprise as a result of all your excellent marketing, and leave without having been sold anything, your great electronic cash register wasn't worth a darn.

The basics of selling bicycles in a retail environment are in this book. There are other books recommended in the appendix that will give you additional sales training. Somewhere in your neighborhood are offered clinics, seminars, and classes on the subject of selling. Invest your time in as many of these as you can.

## Reason #3 - You PLAN the Work - Then Work the PLAN

My Dad greatly enjoys working with wood. I was never any good at it, but he tried to teach me anyway. The clearest lesson he taught was "measure twice and cut it once." I feel confident that every reader is nodding their head at that one. However, the damage from an errant cut on a stick of lumber may, at its worst, amount to ten or twenty dollars and a trip to the lumber yard.

How is it then, that not as many heads start nodding at the notion that you must plan every aspect of your business in detail prior to execution. The errant cutting in this case could mean the loss of your business and all the time, effort, and money that has gone into it.

Chapters 2 and 3 deal with goal setting and planning. Chapter 12 will tell you how to compare your results to the plan, and make adjustments accordingly.

## Reason #4 - You Buy Low, Sell High and Make MARGINS

There is no business principle more steeped in common sense than "Buy Low, Sell High." Unfortunately, few bicycle retailers practice either the "buying low" or the "selling high" parts.

The most successful stores may have <u>started</u> the business with some barn-burner prices to gain market share. They commonly use loss-leaders in advertising and promotions. They will also offer blow-out prices to gain a specific inventory, cash, or marketing goal. **However, the rest of the time, they price their product at levels that maximize margins.**

Successful stores also turn what may seem a quick and easy job of "buying" into the precision science of "purchasing." Purchasing includes the careful evaluation of price, delivery, and terms, but even those are often given short shrift by the harried buyer. However, the real opportunities in buying come from decisions on lines, assortments, receiving, reporting, and creative sourcing. Chapter 9 will reveal common sense practices that can make the difference between running a business to pay the landlord and running one to pay yourself.

## Reason #5 - You Use Creativity in MARKETING

I have seen bicycle shops that have reached a reasonable degree of success by following a plain vanilla approach to marketing. However, the great successes have in common the development of a unique and creative marketing strategy. The approach to marketing store, product, and services can be as simple and inexpensive as putting on well-planned and interesting Saturday morning rides, or as complex, expensive, and time- consuming as advertising on cable television.

Discussed in detail in chapters that follow, the following elements of the business are possible targets for innovative ways to get more folks in and sell them more when they arrive:

1.  Location
2.  Storefront

3. Outdoor signs
4. Outdoor advertising (billboards, bus benches, etc.)
5. Window treatment
6. Yellow Page advertising
7. Interior design
8. Interior signage, merchandising, and brochures
9. Store layout
10. Events, rides, and clinics
11. Other advertising
12. Sponsorships, clubs, and community involvement
13. Cross promotions and mailers
14. Newsletters
15. Public relations

This list could go on for pages, but if you implement any two or three of the above in a creative way, you will greatly increase your chances for success.

## Reason #6 - You do a Good Job of ACCOUNTING for Your Business

It is quite possible to be very successful at bringing in lots of dollars, creating mind-numbing levels of activity, and becoming your supplier's best customer, and yet never earn a profit. If your accounting controls are not in place, you may feel like you're making money when you're not. Without proper financial reports, you are likely to learn the truth too late.

Successful shops are already using POP cash registers, fully integrated computer systems, and accounting methods designed to monitor sales, margins, purchase requirements, cash flow, and earnings. They utilize checks and balances in handling all aspects of the paperwork that reduce opportunities for employee fraud, theft, or mere negligence. Chapters 11 and 12 offer the latest in approaches to these business-saving ideas.

## Reason #7 - You Act in a PROACTIVE Manner

There are certain questions that are constantly dancing through the mind of the successful bicycle shop owner. For example: How many sixth grade students are there in the elementary schools in your service area? How many fifth graders? Fourth? Third?

Is there a major employer in your area that is experiencing hard times? Is there a new business coming to town that will be employing large numbers of workers that are younger, older, lower or higher paid, more home grown or immigrant than is usually true?

Is your neighborhood deteriorating or building? Is your street becoming more, or less, important? Are the politics in your area becoming more pro business or less so?

Where is the bicycle business headed? Will clothes fade or become the rage? Will touring and racing bikes be back? Why or why not?

These questions come from an insatiable desire to learn as much as possible about those things effecting the operation of the business. Reading, attending trade shows, involvement in business clubs and associations, and networking of information through contacts in and outside the trade are the resources for this knowledge.

Having evaluated trends in population data, economics, politics, and local business conditions, the owner can make informed decisions about how to avoid potential pitfalls and take advantage of budding opportunities. Taking action in advance of necessity is "proaction." Those who respond only when necessity forces them to are "reactive."

The proactive dealer also carefully evaluates the various elements of the business for opportunities to head off problems and increase success. The reactive dealer is always under stress as he moves from crisis to crisis.

# CHAPTER 2

# PERSONAL GOAL SETTING

Those who have goals VERY commonly ACHIEVE them. And the converse is true as well: **Those who have no goals can not possibly achieve a goal they have not made.** Thus, the first loss for those who do not make goals is that they cannot enjoy the thrill of achievement.

**Those who have goals VERY consistently ACHIEVE success at a level ten times or greater than those who don't.** A study of Harvard graduates concluded that the mere writing down of your goals creates an increase in lifetime achievement and wealth of ten to one-hundred times those who do not.

In other words, let's say that without goals you might achieve a maximum income someday of $40,000 per year in today's dollars, and that you might eventually enjoy a net worth of $150,000. Most folks would consider that to be a pretty decent result.

If you were to create a clear set of goals and commit them to writing, you would almost certainly reach an income of $400,000 per year and a net worth of at least $1,500,000. This is not a guess. This result has been proven by empirical, scientific studies.

**Those who set goals attain greater peace of mind, have less anxiety, and enjoy life far more than those who don't.** Everybody sets some goals. A goal may be as simple and short-term as, "I want to leave the shop by 6:00 tonight." It might be a bit more long-term and complicated, such as, "I want to get away for a weekend with my wife to a secluded mountain cabin before Christmas."

Goals may involve an ongoing situation where the goal must be constantly met. An example might be, "I want to spend at least two hours per day with my kids." Finally, it might be very long-term and elaborate as, "I want to retire from the bicycle business by age 55, turn over the operation to my children, and move to a golf course condo in Arizona."

As you write down more and more of these types of goals, your future begins to have structure. As you put meat on the bones of these dreams by creating strategies for achievement, you give the goals reality. And, as you make decisions between competing desires and opportunities in your life, you simplify your future path.

It is not difficult to achieve these three great benefits of goal setting. It doesn't take a huge investment of time or energy. It does require some deep soul-searching in an effort to get in touch with your innermost feelings. The following approach is based on an eight-week seminar series I have conducted that has achieved a 97% success level in motivating people from every walk of life to write down their goals.

## WHO ARE YOU?

The first step in setting goals is to determine where you are right now. It isn't going to be very useful to set goals that are not consistent with your abilities or interests. It would be crazy for me to set a goal of becoming the most famous soprano opera singer in the world. In looking at my age and musical talent, I would already have to question such a goal. Then, when reminded of my gender, it takes the idea from the ridiculous to the sublime.

Therefore, begin by determining your personal current assets and liabilities. You could call such a listing a personal inventory. Take a hard look at who you really are. What are your attributes and how can they be maximized and utilized for success? Where do you fall short? Are you an excellent organizer, mechanic, and manager of people? However, you consider yourself to be a poor salesman, a procrastinator, and weak on budgeting?

Don't stop with business skills. Consider every aspect of your life. How do you measure up IN YOUR OWN EYES, not in the eyes of others, on such subjects as friendliness, patience, spirituality, looks, health, athletic ability, leadership, parenting, grooming, special skills? Write as long a list as possible. You may wish to divide the list into positives and negatives. Be honest with yourself. Take a hard, deep look at your innermost being.

Now evaluate that list. Which of the negatives cause you enough concern to want to change them? The rest, forget! One way to create a real boost in peace of mind and positive mental attitude is to decide that there are things about yourself that you want to change, and have enough desire to make the change. Almost as important to the joy of life is deciding that other things you may not like about yourself are acceptable to you, and that you will not make any immediate effort to change these.

Spend at least an hour with this effort to evaluate who you are. Think about it for a week. You would do well to mark this book at this time, put it down, and come back after you have completed your personal inventory.

## WHAT DO YOU WANT?

I have tried my hardest on several occasions to imagine a person who would get in their car, loaded down with family, suitcases, and the like, and set off on a journey without any clue as to where they were going. I have talked to a few folks headed toward retirement who talk about buying a motor home and just setting off. However, in every case, when the time comes to "just set off," out come the maps, the decisions about destinations, the plans of what to see and do.

Then I talk to an owner of a small business. How much do you expect to sell this year? What is your goal for five years from now? How much do you expect to profit? When will you add a second salesperson? Are you planning to open a second store?

If I were to turn to aspects of their personal life the questions might be: Do you want your kids to go to college? What plans do you and your spouse have for you as a couple once the kids are all moved out? What will you do with your time after retirement? Do you have any plans for community service? What are your goals for building better relationships with family, friends, and God?

Only a few have any ideas on these subjects. Fewer yet have created any type of "plan." Almost none can answer the question: "WHY?" or "WHY NOT?"

The second stage of goal setting is to get in touch with the hidden "you" and try to come up with a list of NEEDS, WANTS, AND DESIRES. My personal definition and differentiation of these would be as follows.

A **need** is something we cannot do without. However, it goes beyond mere food, water, or air. We have all developed needs for material things which, were we to lose them, we would feel a certain level of hardship.

Therefore, most folks do need a car, and would consider it a hardship to use public transportation (or heaven forbid, a bicycle). Most of us today would feel underprivileged if we could not afford a 25 inch TV, other entertainment equipment, and a decent home to put them in.

We also have very substantial needs in the areas of relationships, approval, and things spiritual. How many people have spent twenty-five years building their business to great success, only to have their kids drop out and their spouse move out? Failure to think ahead and PLAN a balanced approach to our life may result in great success in one area that is made quite hollow by our tragic failure in another.

**Wants** are the things we buy with discretionary income. It would be nice to have all of our wants filled, but we don't sense any real feeling of loss when we can't quite achieve them. I **want** new computer furniture for my office. I want my kids to listen to me. I want to owe no debt to any man. I can live my whole life without achieving any of these wants. I will not be greatly affected by my inability to get them. However, it would be a plus if they were to happen.

A funny thing about wants is that they are generally a stepping stone between needs and desires. I **need** something to set my computer on if I am to use it at all. I **want** to buy a special unit that will increase my productivity, decrease my fatigue, and look attractive. However, if I were to satisfy this want, it is very likely that a new one would take its place. Either I would now want a new computer, or I might want an even better table.

My kids might begin to listen to me, but very likely I will think of new things I want them to do. I might get out of debt, but now want a portfolio of $1,000,000 in securities.

**Desires** are the real stuff of which goals are made. Generally, they are the ultimate in a list of **wants**. I have always **desired** to have a special room totally devoted to home entertainment. Today I have a multi-purpose room that includes several excellent home entertainment devices, and I currently **want** surround sound with pro-logic. I still **desire** this seperate "room" that would include the complete integration of audio, visual, game, and other equipment . . . and, of course, all leading edge.

The most important advice you will read in this book is to **WRITE DOWN THE DESIRES OF YOUR HEART IN THE FORM OF LIFETIME GOALS!** It isn't very hard, nor does it take that much time. You can probably put together a fairly comprehensive list within an hour or two. The hitch is that it has to be honest, heartfelt, and real.

This list can also include your business goals. However, Chapter 3 will take a deeper look at this subject.

## WHAT'S IT WORTH TO YOU?

This next section will not be of much value to those who have not written down their goals. Based on evidence gathered from several sources, it is unlikely that more than 3% of those reading this book have written down their life's desires.

Let me take one more shot at trying to convince each and every reader to stop reading, set aside everything else you are doing, go find a quiet place where they will not be interrupted, and *set your goals*. According to widely available statistics, only 3% of the population will reach 65 years of age with more than Social Security and/or other company or government pensions for income. Isn't it interesting that the 3% statistic keeps popping up? It is not coincidental.

If you feel as though you would really like to set your goals but need more help to do so, here are two possible solutions:

1.   In February of 1993, you will be able to purchase a copy of my next book, *When Friday Isn't Payday.* This book will be of value to any bicycle shop owner. It includes a comprehensive goal setting plan. Call Info Net Publishing for a copy or purchase one in your local bookstore.

2.   Now available is the eight-week course mentioned above for goal setting and leadership training seminars on audio tape. These also can be purchased through Info Net Publishing.

If you have written down your goals, it is time to evaluate them in terms of how much you want them. It is one thing to say that you have a goal of earning $200,000 per year. It is quite another to devote the time, energy, and money to reach that result.

One of the biggest stumbling blocks is competition between various needs, wants, and desires. You can really desire to spend more time with your kids. Unfortunately, Monday-night football gets in the way. Then there's Thursday-night football, and all-day-Sunday  football.

Another area of conflict can arise from the competing needs, wants, and desires of your family, partner, or friends. As you review your goals, it is a good idea to make certain that those who are important to you are in agreement with your priorities . . . or at least accepting of them.

## WHAT NEXT?

Once the goals are in place, there are two steps to implementation: organization and visualization.  The mere writing down of a goal has tremendous power for creating success.  However, for maximum effectiveness, these other two steps are necessary.

## Organization

Purchase a quality notebook.  It could be of the spiral bound variety or a three-ring binder type. It should be nice enough that it will last for twenty years or so.

Use the first several pages to rewrite you personal inventory list. You might use the first page for assets, the second page for liabilities, and the third page to list those things about yourself that you would like to improve. (You should want to improve assets as well as to change liabilities.)

The next page might be used to list as many goals as come to mind: big ones, little ones, short and long term ones, fanciful and practical ones.

An alternative method would be to use about eight pages for the listing of goals. Each page would represent a different category. For instance, these categories might include spiritual, vocational, marital, familial, recreational, financial, relational, and those involving community.

For this part of the exercise, write fast and free. Don't analyze each item at this point as to the likelihood you will actually pursue it. You should end up with between fifty and one-hundred different goals. If you have less, you may want to spend some more time dreaming. If you have more, that's great.

When you are satisfied that you have completed your list or lists, go through each item and rate it either A, B, or C. This ranking should be based on the importance of the goal and your belief that you can accomplish it. You may also find yourself scratching some items off the list as you do the evaluating.

The next step is to create a plan or strategy for each goal. Move to the next clean sheet in your notebook and write one of your most important "A" goals at the top of the page. Think through each step that will be necessary to achieve the stated goal. You may wish to use a pencil for this effort, as all the steps may not be apparent at first.

Once you have a strategy laid out, go back and put a completion date next to each step in the plan. Once you have plotted this out with a time line, you will now be able to put a date on the goal itself.

Some goals are ongoing. I may want to keep my weight under 140 pounds. For this type of goal there is no completion date. In this case the strategy may or may not have completion dates.

As you proceed with a plan for each objective, you will begin to see the clash of interests. There just isn't enough time in the day. You may also have two or three things that would require singleness of purpose and substantial emotional energy. As these come up, you will have choices to make. In some cases you may wish to put off important dreams until another time in your life. In others, you may just decide you can't have it all, and now is as good a time as any to discard some things.

## Visualization

During the Viet Nam War a soldier who was taken prisoner in one of those famous Viet Cong bamboo cages stumbled onto an important new approach to learning. To keep himself from going crazy, he daydreamed about his favorite peacetime activity, golf.

In this fantasy, he saw himself playing the courses he knew so well. Having plenty of time on his hands, he imagined every detail of his play, from taking the ball and appropriate club out of his bag, to watching his shot soar down the fairway. Day after day he repeated this process.

After his release he expectantly returned to his game. Amazingly, he was playing at the same skill level as before his imprisonment. His **visualization** of playing the game was as beneficial to his ability as actually being on the links.

His experience confirmed what many motivational writers had been saying for years, but had no scientific evidence to back them up: "What the mind of man can **perceive** and believe, it can achieve." Our minds have only limited ability to differentiate between what we actually do and what we imagine that we do. Thus, we often find our emotions in total turmoil over fears, worries, or disgruntlement with things that we imagine might happen in the future, but that, in fact, never do occur.

I suggest that you use this ability in a positive way. Take each goal that you plan to begin work on and daydream about it. Imagine each step of the process to achievement. Enjoy the excitement of each success along the way. See yourself hurdling over the obstacles and side stepping those who stand in your way. Fantasize about your final victory and all the benefits that come with success.

Try to bring all your senses to this visualization party. If your goal is to win the Race Across America, smell the flowers in the bouquet you're handed at the finish line, hear the roar of the crowd, and feel your sweetheart's arms around you.

You will want to return to this "movie" many times as you work towards the goal. As you play the VCR in your head over and over, the tape becomes a part of you, and your mind has already trained for what it has to do.

In addition to visualization, you may also want to use **cut outs** and **self notes** as aids to reaching your heart's desires. Cut outs are just what they sound like. Cut out pictures that represent your goal. If possible, find a picture that exactly states your dream. For instance, you may have a type of house in mind. Look through magazines and newspapers until you find a picture that looks like the perfect dream home.

Cut this picture out. You may wish to paste this into a wish book. This could be the same book where you have been writing down your goals, or it could be another scrapbook specifically designed for pictures.

You may prefer to put the cut out in a place where you'll see it every day. You could tape it to your bathroom mirror, or attach it to your refrigerator door. This latter option is an especially good place to put up a picture of a "thinner" you to help in reaching a weight loss goal.

Self notes are a variation of the same theme. In this approach, you write down a reminder to yourself and put it somewhere you will see it often. If you were interested in sticking to a budget or becoming debt-free you could put a self note in your wallet. Be certain to put it on brightly colored paper so that it jumps out at you each time you start to spend money you haven't budgeted.

A Few Final, and VERY IMPORTANT, Thoughts on Goal Setting.

1.  A reminder: Only 3% of the population write down their goals:

Those who do are at least ten times as successful in life as those who don't. If you've just been reading along in this chapter, agreeing with everything, but not doing anything, THINK!! If you don't stop now and force yourself to take action on thinking about and writing out your hopes and dreams, you probably never will. Opportunity rarely knocks twice. Come on! Take a chance! Go back to the beginning of this section and work through the process!

2. Don't allow fear of goal setting to paralyze you. Only losers will second guess you for failing to reach a goal. You will be the one to second guess yourself for having never set any goals.

   It is perfectly normal to change goals once they're set. As you mature, and as life situations change, it would be more surprising if all your plans stayed the same. However, each time a change is made, it should be done with the same evaluation and thoughtfulness as when it was set originally.

3. The pathway to success is generally paved with the footstones of our failures. Henry Ford was bankrupt twice as a car manufacturer before he founded Ford Motor Company. Edison had more than 1,000 failures on the road to inventing the light bulb. Abraham Lincoln was considered to be less than successful as a lawyer and lost several elections before becoming one of the United States' most revered Presidents.

There are two important attitudes to hold concerning failed efforts. As we approach any new goal, we should expect to succeed. It is critical that we not only **"perceive"** but **"believe"** we can reach our destiny. However, even as we are convinced of our ability to get to victory, we should recognize that it is possible that we will fail. In this way, when we do have setbacks or even a complete miss, it will not shut down our ability to bounce back. Therefore, expect to succeed, but know that there will be failures.

Second, ultimate success in life depends on our ability to get back on the horse after falling down. Each fall should represent a lesson. We learn far more from an error than we do from doing things right. When we hit the bullseye, we now figure we know how to do that, and move on. Sometimes, we really do have the skill well in hand. Other times we are merely kidding ourselves.

However, when we miss the target, we gain valuable data about how to aim next time. If we use this new data intelligently, we will slowly but surely increase the number of hits. Quite clearly, though, if we give up after the first miss, we are the biggest loser of all.

4.  Once an individual sets a goal and writes it down, the rest is remarkably easy. Unfortunately, there is one additional pitfall that needs to be discussed. It is common for a very "successful individual" to end up empty and unhappy. This is generally due to one of the following:

    A. They allow the goals to "own them". There are many kinds of slaves and masters in the world, but one of the worst masters is yourself. When your need for money, fame, power, or recognition rules your life, you will be miserable indeed.

Each goal must be kept in perspective. When you have reached the end of your days, most of your accomplishments will seem unimportant. However, you will likely ask yourself a few questions about how you did with relationships. You will also think about what you contributed to the world.

    B. The goals were too short term. One of my employees told of a goal- setting seminar she attended. The students were required to write down one-hundred goals. She dutifully complied. Three years later, she had accomplished ninety-seven of the one hundred, and found that, instead of exhilarated, she was depressed.

First, all the goals had been material. The teacher failed to understand or communicate that "things" never satisfy. Houses, cars, boats, and jewelry are all beneficial to have, but they never provide a continuing source of satisfaction. After one acquires something, there is always a bigger, better, or more impressive thing to acquire.

Second, there were no long term-goals to keep going after. She completed 97% in three years. It is very common among hard-driving, successful people to find themselves with all their dreams fulfilled and nothing to live for.

17

C. My experience has shown that failure to seek and follow spiritual guidance can doom even the best life design. As we develop our goal list, and begin to develop the strategy for accomplishing each one, our time spent in spiritual reflection will be the most important time of all.

# CHAPTER 3

# YOU'RE NEVER TOO OLD TO MAKE A BUSINESS PLAN

Do you remember when you were growing up or when your own kids were going through various life stages? At a certain age, one is too old for a crib, for training wheels on a bike, or to have somebody always picking up after them.

Some bicycle store owners seem to think that after they've been in business for a while, they become too old to need a plan. This may occur after five years, one year, or even a few months. It's really amazing how early in one's training, some people think they have it all figured out, and need to shed themselves of anything that was useful initially, but now I considered kid's stuff.

Then there are others who never have enough information upon which to base a plan. Another group can't seem to find the time to write down their plans (assuming they've thought about it at all). Yet another group will tell you that planning is worthless, since unknown factors will generally thwart any such effort.

**All such thinking is balderdash and can destroy a viable business.** The more time, thought, and energy you put into the planning process, the better organized you will be. Therefore, you will have more time than ever. The information you need to make valid plans is either at your fingertips or can be. Unknown factors will challenge your ability to make plans a reality, and occasionally cause you to alter them, but it doesn't reduce the value of making plans.

Finally, **planning** is the opposite of kidstuff. It is a valuable tool which produces benefits such as those mentioned above plus planning:

A.  Creates focus
B.  Directs activities
C.  Produces better decision-making
D.  Reduces anxiety
E.  Increases action
F.  Elevates self esteem
G.  Provides a score card
H.  Increases employee productivity

Hopefully, you are now convinced that it would be a good idea to construct a plan for your business. In many cases, there is just one last thing stopping you: Knowing how to construct a business plan.

What follows is the simplest business plan imaginable. If you work through this one, and would like to attempt something more detailed, consider purchasing *When Friday Isn't Payday* for a more comprehensive approach. Or, visit your library for numerous books offering approaches to business planning at any level of complexity you may wish to attack.

## Preparation

Do you have a balance sheet? Do you have an income statement? If not, it is like driving your car down the freeway without dials, gauges, or instruments. Of course, it is possible. However, not knowing your speed, the amount of gas in the tank, oil or water in the engine, or whether your battery is being charged could dramatically alter the success of your journey.

If you don't have these financial reports, take an inventory at the next month end. Add up your payables and see how much you owe. Balance your checkbook. Get together with a CPA or bookkeeper and set up a system for depreciation.

Once you have completed these financial statements (or if you already have them prepared on a regular basis), take a reality check. Are you earning a fair living from this business? Do you get a reasonable return on your investment over and above a decent paycheck? Are you building wealth that will provide you with security in retirement?

Finally, evaluate the non-financial aspects of your business. Here is a list of questions that may help you:

1. How is your location? Is it likely to benefit from the changes you expect in the area? Is it large enough to generate the business you need to reach respectable levels of income and profit? Are you in the right place to serve the customer you are trying to reach? Are you paying too much rent? Do you have security with your current landlord and lease? Should you move?

2. How is your current image? Do you have one in mind? Is your sign helping or hurting you? Are your windows being used as advertising space? Does the overall look of your storefront create awareness and interest? Is your interior attractive, clean, and well-merchandised? Do your employees present a professional image and a customer service attitude? Is your Yellow Page ad and other advertising up-to-date and professionally prepared?

3. How good are your product lines? Do you have the "right" bicycle brands? Are you carrying the clothing, accessories, and parts that your customers need to fully appreciate and enjoy their bicycles? Do you have not enough or too much variety? Are you trying to please too broad an audience? Is your niche too narrow?

4. How are your finances? Do you have reserves in savings? Do you have a banking relationship that allows for short term or long-term borrowing? Do you have good credit relations with your major suppliers?

5. How good are your people? Do your salespeople have a following? Are your mechanics good enough to have a reputation for their work? Is there a spirit of enthusiasm among your employees that goes beyond getting a paycheck?

You may wish to add other questions and answers to the above list. The key thing you want to establish out of this exercise is a basic appraisal of where you and the company stand at this time. If you were about to start out on a ten-day, 1,000 mile bicycle ride, you would check every aspect of bicycle and rider to insure every element was in place to make the journey without incident and with maximum enjoyment and benefit. Doesn't it make sense to do at least as much for yourself and your business, the source of your survival?

## What is Your Niche?

To maximize the potential of any product, service, or business, it is important to identify and seek to fill the needs of a specific market segment in a way that few or no others do. Maybe the best example of a niche player in the bicycle business today is Terry Bicycles, headed by Georgina Terry. No bicycle maker was designing a bike specifically designed to accommodate the different body proportions of women. Terry felt that there could be an entire business built around the concept of filling that need.

You can do the same. Examine the population you serve. Determine the profile of your customer base: Age, income level, family status, most popular uses of free time. Visit city hall or your local chamber of commerce for help in finding statistics.

Next, evaluate the bicycle uses of this population. Are you in a family neighborhood where you might expect heavy usage of a full range of low-to-middle-priced bikes, a university area where students may need pure transportation, or a recreationally-minded community looking for competition equipment?

Think carefully about these issues, and compile as much data as you can. Sometimes, the more you dig, the more surprises you will find. It may be that while you are in a family community, the area is very upscale, and you will sell mostly pricy, name brand products.

Your niche may have less to do with the mix of merchandise than with the services you offer. Maybe the other stores emphasize sales over service. Your specialty could be maintaining the best mechanics in town and the latest in equipment for every kind of repair or upgrade.

You might find that your customers are looking for a folksy store in the midst of high-tech heaven. Or just the opposite.

As an example, look at the trade books in our industry. No one I know questions the idea that *Bicycle Business Journal* enjoys are large part of its success because of the "Partly Personal" column and the generally folksy approach of the Quinns.

Meanwhile, *American Bicyclist* hammers away at product information, and specializes in selling advertising to importers. *Bicycle Dealer Showcase* has consistently offered its readers help in how to run a bike shop. *Bicycle Retailer*, the new kid on the block, focuses on late breaking news.

Each is a trade magazine. Each has the same customer base from which to choose. Yet, each has survived by being as different from one another as possible.

Therefore, the first step in your business plan is to determine what your niche is. Once having determined this in a general fashion, you will want to write it down in what is called a "statement of business purpose." This is a concise statement of what your business does. An example might look like this:

*Tour de Bob's Bike Shop strives to be **the** source for serious, competitive cyclists throughout the three county region. We will do this through maintaining a complete stock of the most desired items, hiring and training highly qualified personnel to sell, and to service what we sell.*

Or:

*Lake Arrowroot Family Bicycle Center's intent is to provide area families with a bicycle shop where they can feel comfortable buying two-wheelers for family members of all ages. Our emphasis will be to provide a friendly atmosphere where children, adults, or seniors will feel welcome.*

Each of these statements establishes the nature of the customer, the approach to the marketplace, and the special way the store intends to appeal to their target customer. You may want to lay this book aside for a moment and consider your statement of business purpose. If you have employees who have been with you a long time, or who you expect will stay with you a long time, you may want to involve them in the process of defining your business purpose.

## What Do You Want for Your Business?

In Chapter 2 we discussed goal setting in detail. The second step in preparing a business plan is to clearly detail what you hope the business will provide you in income, wealth, fame, free time, personal growth, or other dreams you have for the enterprise.

People go into business for themselves for many reasons. In a surprisingly large percentage of cases, bicycle dealers "happen" into business rather than "going" into it. Managers or relatives succeed owners, folks that are out of work start repairing bikes in their garage to eat, or a hobby becomes a business.

The initial reasons for entering business commonly have little to do with what a person would like to get out of it after several years of sacrifice, blood, sweat, and tears. In addition, many owners who have lost sight of what their original reasons might have been, have not replaced these with new purposes.

Your personal goals for the shop may or may not be the same as the business purpose you arrive at. Certainly, you have to sign off and believe in the shop's mission, but your personal needs go beyond those. Here is a check list to get you started in thinking about what you might desire for yourself and your family from this incredibly important asset.

1. **Pay** - Every owner expects to receive some income from the massive effort that is required to run a small business. How should you determine what that income should be? Consider these points:

   A. How much could you be earning as someone else's employee?

   B. What is your contribution to the earnings of the store?

   C. How much would you have to pay to replace yourself?

   D. How much income do you need to pay your personal bills?

24

E.  What dollar figure would make you feel good about your effort?

F.  What is the going rate among owners of similar enterprises?

Taking any or all of these ideas into consideration, are you happy with your current income from the business? What would you like it to be in one year? Two years? Five years? Ten years?

2.  **Return on Investment** - Over and above the amount you take as payment for your personal effort as an employee of the business, you should be expecting to take home additional income to compensate you for the use of your assets in that enterprise. In other words, if you were to sell or liquidate the business tomorrow, you should end up with some amount of cash. If you were to put that cash into a bank account or other investment, what would you earn? How does that compare to the amount you currently receive as a return on investment?

It is possible that you cannot currently take anything out for this category due to the growth of the business. You may be using this money to increase the value of the business, rather than spending it now. If this is the case, then you may want to establish a goal for that increased value. Bottom line: If you are running your shop as a business, you should either be receiving a return on your investment or seeing a growth in the value of the asset.

3.  **Wealth** - Only 3% of the U.S. population will have more than their Social Security and business pension to see them into their retirement years. The majority of humans around the world spend everything they make as fast as, or before, they make it.

One wonderful way to avoid this trap is to be self-employed. Through owning your own business, you should be able to create wealth (assets that are convertible to or produce income) in addition to regular income. When the time comes, you should be able to sell your enterprise. The proceeds should create your escape from a pension reliant retirement.

There are other approaches which can produce this result. You can take the income that you are receiving as your return on investment and reinvest this in other assets (stocks, bonds, real estate, art, currency). This allows you to develop a diversified portfolio of wealth with various levels of risk and liquidity.

One seemingly sure-fire method for building wealth in a bike shop is to purchase the property your shop, or shops, operate from. The mortgage payments will generally be about the same as your rent. Over the years, as the rent goes up in the neighborhood, the mortgage remains the same. At the end of thirty years or less, you have a paid-for piece of property and no rent. Your tax man or lawyer can also advise you as to methods to minimize the tax consequences of this type of approach.

One more way to produce an income stream for your retirement is to sell all or part of the business to an employee, family member, or manager, who then pays you over several years. While this is one of the most common approaches bike shop owners use to convert their shop into earnings, it is the riskiest and takes the most continual involvement.

4.  **Career Satisfaction** - As an owner, what do you want to do for the enterprise? Are you excited by the prospects of managing others, overseeing the ebb and flow of merchandise and money, planning and executing marketing efforts? If you already are an owner, I certainly don't have to tell you that until you have at least four or five employees, you will need to do every job, and sometimes several of them, almost simultaneously.

    The questions to ask yourself at this time are which apects of the business are you best at and which do you like to do? Then it will be possible to plan for the time when you can hire folks to do those things that you like the least or have little aptitude for.

    There is also the question of challenge in your career. In order to be satisfied, do you need to stretch yourself through expansion, through maximizing sales and profit, and/or through becoming better and better at those tasks which you do reserve for yourself? Do you personally thrive through taking on these additional duties?

5.  **Fame or Recognition** - Do you want to use your store and your ownership of it as a platform for personal promotion? I have seen shop owners who have become active politically. Others have gained fame because of the size or distinction of their stores. Still others become leaders in local clubs or in national leadership in the industry.

6.  **Making a Contribution** - For many business owners there is an added awareness of the need for those who have gained greatly from their community to contribute something back. It may be that you are one of these. Therefore, it is important to include in your plan the nature and scope of the contribution of time, energy, or money that you intend to make to your community.

7.  **Free Time** - Are you hoping to work less than eighty hours per week someday? Have you set your sights on sixty, forty, or even thirty? Is it part of your plan to be able to take extensive vacations or even sabbaticals? Whether your need for fewer hours and days on the job stems from a desire to rest and relax or to pursue other dreams, you will want consider these in your planning.

After you have thought through and quantified all of the above, you will be in a better position to flesh out what the business will have to look like to meet those personal goals. Let's take a look at two extremely different examples.

Phillip looks over the above questions about his personal needs regarding his shop, Bicycle In, reviews what he knows about his family's needs and wants, and starts to write down a few thoughts:

*"I look at the bike shop primarily as a source of income that I can control. I like the independence and the risk, but I feel confident in being able to reduce the risk and maintain an excellent business even during tough times.*

*"I need about $30,000 per year to pay my personal bills. I would very much like to make about $50,000, but have no overriding desire to make more than that.*

*"I have few hobbies or other interests, and am not that excited about travel. My family is happy with a two-week vacation each year. Neither*

*my family nor I object to working six, ten-hour days since the shop is only minutes from our house. My wife isn't even too unhappy if I have an hour or two of bookwork at home once or twice a week.*

*"I like to sell, and don't mind at all getting my hands dirty in the repair area. I'm not at all interested in the bookkeeping, but I have enjoyed learning how to use the computer, and that has increased my interest in accounting. I have almost no interest or ability in advertising, promotion, store design, and things like that.*

*"I look at the store as my life-long occupation, and when I retire would like to pass the store on to one of my children if they are interested. If not, I may just run it until I can't move anymore."*

With this set of assumptions, Phil might have a business plan that would include the following elements:

1.  Immediate goal of $300,000 in sales to afford $30,000 salary and still have something left over for growth and savings. Growth is needed to reach eventual goal (within five years) of $500,000 in sales. Savings are needed as buffer against tough years. Goal for savings is $10,000 per year.

2.  To reach $500,000, store will either have to expand or a second store will have to be added. Decision on approach to be reached by end of year two in order to implement by end of year three. Current leaning is towards expansion of current facility. Expansion might include using savings as down payment on property.

3.  Begin effort immediately to find and hire outside consultant for all aspects of store promotion. Make certain there is a clear-cut budget and that results are reviewed. Consultant should know exactly what goals are, so they can be part of the team effort to achieve them.

4.  Make ongoing personal effort to improve skills in selling and sales management. Read, listen to tapes, and attend seminars. Look for highly- skilled, long-term salesmen. This type of salesman, though requiring more income, will assure the kind of long-term continuity Phillip's goals call for.

5.  Find an excellent outside CPA. Make certain that most of the

work is done by the CPA's bookkeeper at $50 per hour or less. Only the most sophisticate bookwork needs to be done by the CPA, himself. For this size business, you shouldn't need a CPA who charges more than $125 per hour. This CPA should analyze the books, not merely compile them. He should give his advice on margins, overhead ratios, inventory levels, record keeping, and other aspects of financial management.

6.  Begin making clear plans by age 50 for succession of interested sons or daughters. It is very important for a smooth and happy transition that there is a completely clear understanding of how a transfer of power and ownership will work.

Now let's take a look at a totally different set up:

Brenda and her partner, Donna, have very big plans for Bicycles Built for You. Their current store is already the largest in its market area with $600,000 in sales. This allows both women to take $35,000 home.

Brenda is married to a tax accountant who makes about the same income, and who does the company's accounting at a reduced rate. Donna is engaged to be married to a produce salesman who works on commission. His income varies from $20,000 in a poor year to $60,000 in a great one.

Donna is the hard charger of the two, but Brenda is very excited by their prospects. They both agree that they would like to build this business to the point where it could be sold or go public. They would ultimately like to retire with enough wealth that they could travel extensively and not have to worry about money. Because of the spouses' second incomes, they are both willing to forego maximizing current income in order to build the business quickly.

Brenda has children at home and needs to limit her on-premises work to about 45 hours per week. She is willing to limit her vacations to one week per year while giving Donna three to balance out her longer work weeks.

For these two the business plan needs to be much more elaborate. It also needs to concentrate heavily on financial management. For rapidly growing companies, cash flow can be the most important factor to consider.

Brenda and Donna's business should be structured as follows:

1. The first figure that should be established is the dollar amount they will each need to retire. It would seem that for their needs, anything less than $2,000,000 each will not provide the kind of lifestyle they are seeking. Therefore, the first goal would be to retire in twenty years with $2,000,000 each.

2. It would seem likely that they will need a minimum of $40,000,000 in sales to interest a buyer, group of buyers, or the public (through a stock offering) in paying $4,000,000 for the business. This seems like a lot, so they could plan to raise half by prudent investment of current income in outside investments. With this in mind, they decide to set up a separate corporation to purchase the properties the bike shops will sit on. The separate corporation will rent the stores to the shop owning company.

   The plan will be to own all the properties free and clear by the twentieth year with a value of $2,000,000.

   Therefore, they now figure that if they have twenty stores with real estate values averaging $100,000 each and sales averaging $1,000,000 each, they will have their goal. This seems more attainable.

3. They now need to bring that number forward. They plan to open one store per year for the first five years, and two stores per year in the sixth through twelfth year.

4. Donna and Brenda also must divide the responsibilities. It is decided that Donna will concentrate on sales and promotions, while Brenda will work more closely with administration. Neither is very knowledgeable about running a service section, and while their current manager is doing an excellent job, they feel he is maxed out overseeing the one shop. They make an immediate goal of hiring an expert who will hire and fire personnel, and manage the chain's service departments.

   Review the above examples as you consider your own business plans. You may want to find a quiet spot where you can think about what you want to get out of the effort you are now expending and will continue to expend over the years. Once having thought through your desires, commit them to paper.

## How Do You Get There from Here?

After you've established your personal goals, and those of your business, you are now in a position to determine the details of the strategy to accomplish those goals. Following are some considerations in determining those details:

A. Sales - What dollar amount of sales will you need each year to reach your goal for the fifth year, tenth, or twentieth? Now break down those goals as many ways as you can. How many dollars per month? Are you seasonal? Then you need to show the skew of your sales with monthly estimates.

What percentage of sales will be bicycles? Accessories? Service? If you plan to have more than one location or if you have several salespeople, estimate the sales by location or by salesperson. Don't forget to take into consideration the likelihood of future recessions. Figure in those slow years in determining how well you'll have to do in the good years to make the eventual figure.

B. Location - Will your present location be satisfactory for your future plans? Will you need to move, expand, redecorate, or open more locations? How will you make these decisions? Write out clear strategies for location selection that include such considerations as size, neighborhood, rent, traffic, length of lease, availability of purchase, codes and restrictions, proximity of competition, and availability of important bike lines.

C. Advertising and Promotion - How will budgets be determined? What are the most likely venues to be used? What will be the emphasis and approach? Who will be the target? How will effectiveness be measured?

What unique promotional opportunities are available to you to stand out from the competition?

D.  Organizational Structure - What will your staff organization look like? How many employees will you need at various sales levels? If there will be seasonal hiring, how many people, and for what period of time? What will be methods and levels of compensation and benefits?

E.  Financial - What will be the margin goals in each department? Overall? What percentage of sales will be acceptable for overhead? What is the anticipated before tax profit? Will outside lending sources be necessary? Are those in place? Will current lending limits be adequate? If not, what levels will be needed, and when?

You will do yourself a big favor if you construct a month by month projection of earnings for at least twelve months out. The second twelve months could be by quarter, although the best plans cover two years, by month. You can get one format for such a plan from your bank. You could ask your accountant to create one for you. In Chapter 12, "Bike Shop Finance," I will show you how to construct a computerized projection that provides both an estimate of earnings as well as a cash flow analysis.

F.  Purchasing - What basic product lines, brands, and depth for each will you carry? What margin requirements do you have for each category or line? What dollar amount or unit amount of inventory will you maintain? This should be a function of marketing and cash availability.

Who will do the purchasing? How much authority will they have? Will you use formal purchase orders? (The correct answer is, "yes!")

G.  Systems - At what point in the life of your shop will you have a fully integrated hand bookkeeping system? When will you move into computers? What kinds of future upgrades to these systems do you foresee? What kind of learning curves do you anticipate for you and your staff in implementing each new system.

Major Expansion - Will you be considering other major lines of business for your existing location or locations? Will you be expanding any current locations? Will you be moving any locations to larger quarters? Will you be opening new units?

As you answer these questions, write up a formal report as if you were selling the business to a new owner or to the bank. You would want them to see exactly where you are going and what your strategy is intended to accomplish. You can use an outline, a narrative style, or just list things by the numbers. Whatever approach you use, it should show a clearly defined path from where you are to where you're going. Of course, once you have completed this effort, you may actually have the need to show it to a bank or a buyer. You will now be prepared to do so.

## What Next

A major benefit of writing a thorough business plan is just doing the exercise itself. By gathering the information, accessing and evaluating the possibilities, and writing everything down, you will provide vital benefits to your ability to manage.

However, to derive even greater results, use this document as a check list. As you progress from month to month, quarter to quarter, and year to year, evaluate your results against your plan. Use the disparities to make changes in the plan or in the strategy as appropriate. Re-evaluate and update the plan regularly.

Beware of allowing the plan to drive the business. When special situations or opportunities arrive, see how they fit into the plan, but be prepared to throw out the plan if the new prospects warrant. A plan is a tool to be used by its owner, not a millstone to be worn about the neck.

Share all or part of the plan with your spouse, employees, accountant, suppliers, and banker. You can instill a great measure of confidence in your future prospects by showing these partners in your business that you have a well-designed plan.

Best I Can Tell, It Says:
'Nothing Happens Until Something is Sold!'

# CHAPTER 4

# SALES FUNDAMENTALS FOR BICYCLE DEALERS

It is my hope that if I leave only one legacy from my combined writing and speaking over the years, it would be the importance of sales professionalism in the retail bicycle store. The fact that bike shops still retain some romantic aspects of their "mom and pop" past does in no way lead to the proposition that salesmanship is not allowed. As we enter the 21st Century, I can predict one thing for certain: Those owners who do not learn to sell . . . will not survive.

In my twenty some years in the bicycle industry, I have seen hundreds of new shops open and even more close. It has been a rare occurrence indeed where the store went out of business because too many bikes were being sold. You can make mistakes in location, hiring, store layout, purchasing, or bookkeeping and keep the business going with enough sales. However, the most beautiful store in town on the very best corner will surely fail if the folks inside don't turn a high percentage of shoppers into buyers.

The next few chapters will provide you with everything you will ever need to know about selling in a bicycle shop. There would be much more to learn if you were selling insurance, computers, or Boeing 797's. And, I am not going to give you any academic nonsense, psychological poppycock, or lists of anecdotes about successful salesfolks. If you want to learn more, however, I will provide you with a long list of authors and books on sales techniques.

Some of these are what I would consider highly recommended, and will do much to embellish what follows.  Beyond these classic works, however, it seems to me that much of what is written on selling would tend to fuzz up the issues, and lead to a loss of focus on the fundamentals.  The most successful college basketball coach of all time, John Wooden, had it right, when he constantly encouraged the UCLA basketball Bruins to stick to the fundamentals.

## Three Sales Myths

To begin with, let's examine and put to rest three attitudinal myths regarding sales and selling.

Myth #1. *Salesmen are born to sell.* This proposition just isn't so.  Most stereotypes have their basis in reality, and there are certainly those individuals who are blessed with good looks, large stature, excellent verbal skills, and easy charm that may decide to use those natural gifts to pursue a sales career.

However, these seeming advantages have about as much to do with success in selling as good looks do in predicting whether someone will make a good husband or wife.  Give me an individual who desires to succeed, and who is willing to follow the basic sales fundamentals, and I will build you a salesman.

A close friend of mine has constantly been a top performing salesman in a company that employs thousands of sales professionals.  He is below average height, a member of an ethnic minority, and the son of immigrants.  Many years ago, in my continuing effort to determine what key ingredients were needed to produce a superstar salesperson, I asked him what books, tapes, mentors, or other aids he had used to build his abilities.

He was really quite puzzled at first, and asked me to help him understand more clearly what I was requesting.  I explained that I had read every book I could get my hands on having to do with improving my techniques, attitudes, and methods.  In addition, I had attended seminars, played tapes, and studied the lives of famous salesmen.  What I was hoping he would add to my understanding was his own personal secret.

After a bit of pondering on his part, a light seemed to go on in the recesses of his memory. "Well," he said, "when I first started with the company, they gave us a training manual. I read that and followed it exactly. It seemed to me that they had built this company and that they would know how to become successful with their product."

SELLING IS HARD!! The main reason it's hard is that in order to do it well, you have to follow the basic training manual. The rules are not hard to learn. Each of them is quite easy to perform. Unfortunately, most new sellers are not exposed to the manual, and of those who are, many believe they have a better way. There isn't! And there won't be! These principles have been the basis for selling success throughout history, and it is very unlikely they will change in your lifetime.

Selling is not something you are born to do. It is a learned profession. Anyone who is willing to learn a set of principles and follow them can become very successful as a salesperson.

Myth #2. *Most people feel that salespeople are obnoxious or worse.* One of my favorite things about the human condition is **irony**. It is so interesting to me that if you swing any bat, racket, or stick too hard in an attempt to strike any ball, you will generally end up with less success than when you use a solid, even swing.

It is very much like this in selling. The obnoxious salesman is **not** a professional. He is generally self-trained, lacking in self esteem, and desperate for the next sale. As a result, he will commonly come off as pushy, loud, and self centered.

A trained salesperson will generally be among the best-liked individuals in any group. They have been trained to listen carefully for peoples' needs. They inject excitement and enthusiasm into any conversation or project. They exhibit a sense of purpose, and seem confident of their abilities. Stop and think about some of the professional salespeople you know: the insurance agent who provides your commercial coverage; the representative from your most successful clothing vendor; the saleperson who helped you locate and rent your store.

Myth #3. *Selling is neither a profession nor career, and isn't a very highly paid job.* There are many people employed in sales who are neither professional nor are they planning to make selling a career. However, there are also countless others who are as serious and dedicated to learning the business of sales as any doctor, lawyer, or accountant.

As to the potential financial rewards, there is no limit to the amount an individual can make in this field. It is also one of the few career choices where the level of earnings is not directly related to formal schooling, age, sex, race, length of time on the job, or any other external criteria. The most critical determinant of income is generally **desire.** Show me a salesperson who wants more than anything else to become successful, and you will generally find someone who quickly earns in the top 5% of all wage earners.

## A SHORT SELLING COURSE FOR BICYCLE DEALERS AND THEIR STAFF

The following principles of selling can be your training manual for success in selling bicycles and related equipment and service. Much of what follows could be used with only minor changes for selling Avon or Patriot Missiles, but has been written specifically for the bicycle retail environment.

## THE FIRST FUNDAMENTAL - BE ENTHUSIASTIC

When you are in the process of selling a bicycle, you are generally entering a dialogue that will result in the customer spending about two weeks of hard earned money at your shop. They will commonly be spending more than they would for a television, a sound system, or a monthly car payment, a substantial expenditure of hard-to-come-by, discretionary cash.

Before handing over the VISA, they are going to want to believe that they are making the right decision. Their belief will come from a judgment that they will make about YOU, YOUR STORE, AND YOUR PRODUCT. Therefore, **If you are not enthusiastic about yourself, your store, and your product, WHY would you expect the customer to be so?**

Your enthusiasm will generally have more to do with your success or failure in selling each customer than any of the other elements that follow, except possibly "closing." From the very moment that you begin a dialog with a customer, you will begin to make an impression. How sad it is that many retail salespeople feel that they should appear only half-interested when first approached for help in making a selection.

Another group really is only half-interested. They consider consumers to be "boobs" who don't know much about bikes, and who waste the clerk's time with stupid questions. Then they wonder why so many folks walk out of the store without a purchase.

Everyone has heard that **the customer is KING.** It is the customer who pays the salaries, the rent, and provides the profit. When a customer visits our company, AC International, we generally pull out all the stops to make them feel very special. We have been know to actually roll out a red carpet. We have created welcome signs with a cutout of Snoopy holding a sign welcoming the customer by name.

What are some things that you can do to create enthusiasm in your presentations, in the store, and in yourself?

A.  Why not greet each customer with a smile, (You will be amazed to find that 80% to 90% will smile back.) a handshake, and an exchange of names? It will seem difficult and hard the first few times, but you will be amazed at the effect, and at how quickly it will seem as natural as "may I help you" seems now.

B.  If you can't bring yourself to try "A" above, at least drop "may I help you" in favor of "WHAT KIND OF BICYCLE ARE YOU LOOKING FOR TODAY?" You see, the first approach can be answered with a "no," or an "I'm just browsing." The second approach is much more likely to open a dialogue.

From time to time you will be rejected with a comment such as "I'm just browsing." However, because of the way you began the conversation, you will find it easy to continue to probe with a question such as "Were you thinking along the lines of a mountain bike or a road bike?"

C.  With a genuinely cheerful attitude, take every opportunity to boost your store, your product, and yourself. If the customer indicates he is interested in mountain bikes, you might mention that your store carries the largest stock in town, that you sponsor a team that has had recent success, or that you personally enjoy the sport.

D.  When showing products, do what you can to make the presentation animated and involve the customer as much as possible. To show the smooth working of the gears, you might pick up the back of the bicycle, spin the crank, and allow the customer to work through the gears. Ask the prospect to roll the bike forward and then apply the brakes to get a feel for how it will react.

When conducting seminars on this subject, those in attendance commonly agree that it isn't always that easy to be enthusiastic. On a rainy day in April, when the first customer walks in at 4:30 in the afternoon, you may have had much of your enthusiasm leak out during the past few hours.

We've all had days when everything's going wrong, or when we don't feel that hot. How do we get "Up" for days like that? For most salesmen, the answer is: "**Act** enthusiastic and you will **be** enthusiastic."

In order for you to be enthusiastic for every customer, I recommend that you come up with your own version of the bell. You might use the bell or buzzer on your door that announces that a customer has just arrived. Whenever you hear your cue, you will begin to smile, energize yourself, and act in an enthusiastic manner.

You will be amazed to see that by acting in this way, you will quickly begin to feel much better. Your mood will imitate your action. The next thing that happens is that your customer's mood will imitate yours. In turn, you will be encouraged by his reaction to your upbeat manner, with an additional improvement in your own attitude.

Your enthusiasm should flow naturally from the introduction into the product presentation. It should automatically cause you to concentrate on the features and **benefits** of your products or services, rather than making the mistake of dealing in the negatives of either your own offerings or those of your competition. It is very hard to be negative when you are enthusiastic.

One of the most famous motivators of this century was Dale Carnegie. You have undoubtedly heard of one or more of his books, such as *How to Win Friends and Influence People,* and *How to Stop Worrying and Start Living.* He also developed the most successful public speaking and self improvement course in the USA which carries his name.

An important fundamental idea proposed by Carnegie in his books and courses is that you will be more interesting to others on subjects about which you are well-versed. I'd like to take this concept one step further. It is far easier to make an enthusiastic presentation about a product you know backwards and forwards.

Professional salespeople learn all that they possibly can about everything they sell. You should be constantly reading trade books, consumer magazines, and club mailings to learn about the merchandise you are selling and what is happening in the world of bicycling. You should be looking for every opportunity to pick the brains of sales reps, more experienced staff members, and associates from throughout the industry. If you are well prepared to present the product, you will project confidence and interest, both of which contribute to sales success.

There are a number of additional aids to projecting an enthusiastic attitude. You may have heard everything on this list before, but there is no better teacher than repetition.

1.  Smile - Enthusiasm is contagious, so is smiling. It is even more difficult to be negative when you are smiling than when you are merely enthusiastic. This goes for you during your presentation, and for your customers when they approach a decision.

2.  Compliment your customer - Deliberately look for something about the person that you sincerely find appealing. It might be his name, hair style, outfit, or depth of knowledge about his intended purchase. Don't overdo, and don't settle for a half-

hearted statement about something that you don't truly care about. That will work against rather than for you.

3. If you exchange handshakes, make yours firm and sincere. This is particularly true for men shaking hands with other men. You will be judged mightily on the nature of your handshake. Give another man a limp, wet handshake and you have lost him in the same way you would if you had terrible breath or B.O.

A man shaking a lady customer's hand should allow her to take the lead. If she prefers the dainty, feminine approach, take her hand gently between your thumb and index finger. If she offers a business-type handshake, return it with an equal amount of firmness.

A female salesperson may wish to show her individuality through her handshake with a male customer. She should recognize, however, that a certain percentage of her customers may be slightly offended by too aggressive a shake from a young woman.

In every case, the effectiveness of the handshake can be doubled or tripled through the use of your other hand. Bring the free hand around and grasp the person's hand, forearm, or shoulder to greatly increase the warmth of the greeting. Combine this with a genuine smile, and you will be miles ahead with your prospect.

Hopefully, you have begun to realize how important enthusiasm is to the selling business. It establishes a positive environment for bringing about a sale. And, after all, no sale . . . no business.

## THE SECOND FUNDAMENTAL - FIND THE NEED . . . AND FILL IT

The sales professional recognizes that he is not in the business of trying to persuade people to buy products or services. Rather, it is his job to try to match his product or services with his customer's needs.

42

I don't want to pick on anyone unnecessarily, but I have watched or been a part of so many selling situations where the seller began pitching before he had a clue as to what the customer wanted. The customer looks at the price tag on a mountain bike, and the clerk pounces on him with chapter and verse about every cross bike currently in the shop (and a few he expects to get in next week).

A proper presentation is divided into two distinct parts. First the salesman probes the customer's need with a series of questions designed to determine as much as possible about his need. You may wish to memorize some of the following questions related to selling a bicycle:

1. What kind of bicycle do you have in mind?

2. Are you planning to use the bike for recreation or transportation?

3. How did you become interested in cycling?

4. Will you be riding with a group of friends?

5. Have others recommended certain features or brands?

6. What kind of previous cycling experience do you have?

Of course, some of your customers will have a much clearer idea of what they want than will others. For some newcomers to the sport who have not sought the opinions of their friends before coming in, you may need to spend substantially more time probing:

1. Are you familiar with the three primary types of adult bicycles on the market today?

2. Have you used multiple gear bicycles before?

3. Do you prefer to start with a fairly simple piece of equipment now, with the intention of moving up later? Or would you prefer a bicycle that will be satisfying even after three or more years of active use?

Each answer should suggest another question. In less than five minutes you should have been able to narrow the customer's choice to one or two products you carry. Moreover, you have accomplished two other important aspects of the sale.

First, your questions suggest to the prospect that you are genuinely interested in him and his need, not just in making a quick buck. The more sensitive and personalized the questions, the more likely the customer is to perceive your motivation as pure and in his interest.

Second, you have involved the customer in the process. He is helping you to help him make the purchase. By the end of the presentation, he may feel as if the bicycle you selected for him was really all his idea.

Once you have asked enough questions to narrow the options to no more than two, you are ready to begin part two of the presentation- recommending a bicycle that has two or three **features**, whose **benefits** offer **solutions**.

It is another common error of the untrained salesperson to talk only features. They assume that their customer will understand the benefits to be derived from these. But, in fact, the reverse is more likely to be true, especially in the technical and ever-changing world of bicycles. It is not enough to say that this particular cross bike has a certain Shimano derailleur. **If the customer is looking for an answer to a shifting problem**, you would tell him about the particular derailleur and how it will solve his problem.

If it wasn't obvious from the above paragraph, let me emphasize that the opposite is true, also. **If the customer is not looking for a solution to a shifting problem, don't even mention derailleurs.** The key to recommending a particular product after you have gathered the facts is to limit your "pitch" to those aspects which are important to the customer.

In addition, limit yourself even further to the two or three most important solutions.

As long as you are talking about things that the customer cares about - himself, his needs, the solutions to his problems - you will have his attention and you will be moving him along toward a sale. If you decide to show off your knowledge by talking about items the customer doesn't care about, or by throwing in a few extra features because you feel you must overwhelm the customer with reasons to buy, you will take a big chance on losing your momentum.

Besides, if the customer feels that there is an area of need that has not yet been addressed, he is perfectly capable of bringing it up on his own. If there is dead time which seems to stem from the prospect's uncertainty, ask if there are other areas of concern rather than shotgunning whole lists of components and their benefits. If the customer seems to be a little anxious, you may be better off to stop talking or change the subject back to a more general area such as: "Say, have you seen the new bike path they opened where the railroad tracks used to be."

To maximize the interest of the future cyclist at this point in the sale, pull out the bicycle you hope to sell him. Separate it from all the others and bring it to a location where your presentation of the three features and benefits can have the greatest visibility.

Harking back to the first fundamental, "Be Enthusiastic," involve the customer in active demonstrations of the features you're trying to explain. Pause a minute to let him take a breather by sizing him to the bike. These 60 seconds or so when you are not selling, allows your presentation to sink in, and gives the customer a chance to think about any other questions he might have.

## THE THIRD FUNDAMENTAL - HANDLE OBJECTIONS WITH QUESTIONS

If all has gone fairly well, you have now spent a fairly pleasant ten minutes with your prospect. You have been warm, enthusiastic, and listened attentively to your customer's every word. Assuming you have done your job well you should now expect an objection or two.

"WHAT!" you ask. "If I've done my job, there shouldn't be any objections. I hate objections."

**Objections are a salesman's best friend.** They are an indication of interest. If a person has already made up his mind not to buy, he will generally just politely excuse himself and head out the door. The interested party, on the other hand, will raise objections for one of several reasons: He wants to be sure about his decision; he is stalling for time to make a decision; he truly needs to get certain issues on the table to make a clear decision. All three of these motives point to a sale.

However, the way that you react to objections may have a great deal to do with the final result. You need to be every bit as prepared to deal with this part of the sale as any other part. If you stammer and blush, backpedal and give political answers, you could lose the sale and the customer.

The first part of dealing correctly with objections is just realizing that they are your ally, and not your foe. Relax, knowing that you are continuing to move towards the sale. Now, show your true interest and concern in your customer's objection by **asking a question**. Through the question method you are attempting to clarify the exact nature of the objection. In this way, you will be certain to respond to your customer's real concern. You see, some people will throw out an objection that isn't fully thought out, or that is really just a stall. One of my salesmen called these objections "whiskers" because they hide the true problem.

Let's look at a couple of examples:

John:       This looks like a very good bike, but I was looking for a Schwinn.

You:        I remember you mentioned that, John. What was it about the Schwinn that would cause you to prefer it over this one?

John:       Well, it's a name I grew up with. I've never heard of this brand.

By asking a question, you were able to determine that the reason for the objection had to do with the integrity of the brand name. Without asking, you may have spun your gears for five minutes trying to prove the advantages of your brand. Instead, you can now concentrate on providing some background on the factory that made the bike.

Sue: It seems heavy to me.

You: Gosh, Sue! This one is about average in weight. I have lighter ones, but they are more expensive. Is weight an important factor for you?

Sue: Not important enough to pay more for.

Again, it would be so easy to jump on his objection with all kinds of data about different materials, or comparisons with bicycles in the store and brands you don't carry. However, the right question puts this issue to rest, right away.

Bob: I think I saw one that looked just like this over at K-Mart for about $99.

You: You know, Bob, it does look a bit like this one, and it is worth every penny of $99. Would you like me to go over with you, in detail, the dozens of advantages of this bicycle compared to that one?

Bob: Heh, heh. I was mostly kidding.

Note: Never knock the competition. You can really disarm your customer by complimenting your adversary. The issues of price and/or competition on price generally are the greatest problem for the untrained salesperson. In this instance, many retailers would have started using words like "junk," and might have spent five or ten minutes teaching the customer about the differences between department store bikes and ones sold by independent dealers.

However, as before, a well-thought-out question suggests you are truly concerned about his objection, and that you don't want to waste his time if he was not all that serious. If he had reacted to your question in a way that indicated he was very serious, then it would be necessary to go back to the three features and benefits that you discussed before. Compare the discount brand to yours on these three issues only. Then ask: "Do you think these advantages are worth the extra money?" 90% of the time the answer will be "yes."

For the other 10%, you should continue probing.

You:        I certainly understand that getting value for our money is important in these times. I wouldn't want you to spend a nickel more than you have to in order to get a bicycle that will take care of your needs. Are there other aspects of your purchase decision that we haven't discussed yet? For instance: are you handy with tools so that you can handle your own tune-ups and repairs?

Once again, your statement shows that you care, and your question can lead to a short lesson on the long-term costs of owning an inexpensive bike.

As anyone who has spent more than a few days selling is aware, there is an almost endless variety to the possible objections you will get from an interested, buy wary, consumer. However, at the top of the list of those most frequently given is: "It costs too much." While it may be the most common objection, it is also the one that salespeople have the most difficulty dealing with. Therefore, we will spend the balance of this section offering numerous potential responses to: "It costs too much." From these examples you should be able to develop a method of dealing with any type of objection . . . by asking an appropriate question.

Sandy:      Gee! It's kind of expensive.

You:        **Would you like to look at something with a few less features?** I believe this is the right bicycle for your use, and it is an excellent value, but I can show you some other, less expensive, options if you wish.

Alex:       I can get this cheaper at Pedal and Putt down the street.

You:        **Are you certain it is exactly the same item?**

Alex:       Yes. Same brand, same model, same components.

You:        **What price is he offering?**

Alex:       He's ten dollars under you.

You:

(Option 1)  If Pedal and Putt continues to sell bikes at that price, he will soon be out of business. It will be a good deal for

|  | you this one time, but he won't be around for the long haul. **Do you think a store owner deserves a fair profit for his products?** |
|---|---|
| *(Option 2)* | I can't compete with him. I believe that I offer better long-term service for my customers. **Is the ten dollars going to make the difference between buying from me or from Pedal and Putt?** |
| *(Option 3)* | We are not allowed to discount our bicycles, but I can give you a 10% discount on all clothing and accessories you purchase today if you buy the bicycle. |
| Linda: | What kind of discount are you going to give me? (A variation would be, "I'll give you $375 and not a penny more.) |
| You: | I'm sorry, Linda. Our store does not allow discounting. We do give you a free water bottle with your purchase. We have attempted to provide a very fair price for everyone rather than give an advantage to those who are the best bargainers. **Doesn't that seem more fair?** |
| Gary: | I'm just not going to pay $295 for a bicycle that doesn't look much different from the one over at Wal Mart for $129. |
| You: | **Would you pay more for a Cadillac than you would for a Chevy?** |
| Gary: | Sure. |
| You: | **What are some of the reasons you would be willing to pay more?** |
| Gary: | Well, you know, the Cadillac would be more comfortable, better stereo, lots of gadgets, and more prestige. |
| You: | **Plus, you'd probably expect it to give you less trouble, and if you had to have service, you'd probably get better service, right?** (If the light hasn't gone on for this guy at this point, you'll just have to explain it to him.) |

# FUNDAMENTAL NUMBER FOUR -
# SHUT UP AND SELL

Another of those myths that seem to surround the sales business is that selling is about talking. Some less successful salesmen seem to think that the more talking you do the better your chances for success. This is wrong for at least two reasons. First, unless you are an excellent listener, you won't have the slightest idea how to fill your customer's need. Therefore, listening is more important than talking.

Second, and to the point of fundamental four, it is more important to know when to end your presentation than it is to know whether you have said enough. It is only the rare individual in sales who has a problem with talking too little or failing to speak when he should. Besides, the customer will commonly let you know if he needs more information by asking for it. It is, unfortunately, considered impolite to tell a salesman you already know more than you care to know about the decision at hand.

You will want to stop the presentation when you have provided your prospect with three features and benefits that will solve his stated or implied needs and worked through any objections by carefully exploring the real reason for each one. If you continue to sell beyond that point you risk losing the sale for one of several reasons:

1.  INFORMATION OVERLOAD. Have you ever had a customer say to you at the end of your pitch, "Gee, I never knew there was so much to learn about bicycles. I appreciate all that information, but now I need some time to think about all that. I'll be back in a day or two with my decision."

    In a perfect world this would not seem to be such a bad result. You have done the customer a service by educating him about bicycles. He now is able to make an informed choice. Unfortunately, the world is far from a perfect place, and one of the imperfections is the number of opportunities that lie between the door of your shop and his home for him to spend his $395 somewhere else . . . like on a bicycle from another store or out of a catalog . . . or on his bills . . . or maybe on a pair of inflatable tennis shoes.

2.  PLAIN BOREDOM. If you are in a group of people and the subject turns to 14th century composers, does it matter to you how enthusiastic the speaker is, or how much he knows about his subject? You (and I) can hang in there for about five minutes Then your thoughts turn to, "How can I politely get away from here."

Because you are no doubt a cycling enthusiast, you may find this hard to believe, but much of the information that you may find fascinating about a bicycle will be as boring as details about 14th century composers for many who visit your store. Just because they may wish to buy and ride a bike, doesn't mean they would sign up for a symposium on the subject.

3. NO TIME. In today's hustle and bustle world, many folks don't have time to linger over purchases. Adult men, in particular, generally do not care for shopping, and generally wish to find what they are looking for, buy it, and get out.

Many of your customers are visiting your store on a lunch break or as one of a series of errands, and they have limited time to spend on purchases at your store. If you are not sensitive to their needs in this regard, their minds will drift to their next stop, or to the fact that they are running late. Then you may hear: "I'm sorry, but I've got to run. I'll catch you in a few days and we can discuss this further." Fat chance!

4.  UNSELLING. The longer you talk, the more likely you are to create a serious objection. I've stood and watched sales clerks kill perfectly good sales by bringing up a competitive product to make a point. The prospect, who had already decided to buy, now wants to know more about the bicycle that worried the salesman so much he brought it needlessly into the conversation.

In addition to all these potential reasons that you may push the sale out the door, there is also an economic factor at work. The longer it takes you to complete each transaction, the less profit you make. Whether you are an owner, manager, or clerk, your time is costing the company money. For managers, clerks, and some owners, the cost can be seen in actual payroll dollars. For all owners, there is also the question of lost opportunity cost. If you spend half an hour completing a sale that could have been done in twenty minutes, the other ten minutes could have been used to work with another customer, plan a promotion, or handle any one of thousands of other managerial tasks.

## FUNDAMENTAL NUMBER FIVE - TRIAL CLOSE AND CLOSE

In most selling situations, the next step in the process is usually the hardest. The trial close is a method of checking the customer's temperature before asking for the cash. It is the ultimate in soft sell, because it doesn't require a commitment on the part of the customer, and if the answer isn't what the salesman wanted to hear, there is plenty of room to rebound for another try.

There are many possible ways to approach the trial close in every sale, but it does not come naturally. It needs to be a part of an overall strategy. For instance, after you have made the presentation and handled objections, you might ask, "Is this the type of bicycle you had in mind?" Notice, we are using the question approach again.

If the customer says yes, you can move on to the close. If he still has questions, this is the perfect way to give him a chance. If the answer is no, it is easy to ask new questions to determine why you are not filling his need.

This kind of approach will work very well with higher-ticket accessories, clothes, shoes, and the like. However, for the bicycle itself, there is a built-in trial close: "Would you like to take it out on a test ride?" If the customer says yes, and after the ride, you properly close the sale, you will write up more than 90% of those who test ride.

Several dealers who have heard my presentation at Interbike or CABDA workshops have mentioned that, whenever possible, they like to ride with the customer. This accomplishes several beneficial results.

First, it gives the seller an opportunity to instruct the rider in the proper use of gears, brakes, and quick-release hubs. This may pay big dividends in preventing future liability problems.

Second, you may wish to ride along on a "step up" bike. During the ride you could suggest that he try yours to see if he likes it better.

Third, with you along on the ride, you have diminished the likelihood of theft. I know the last time I test road an automobile, I was shocked to have the salesman ride along with my wife and me. When I asked, he finally admitted, it was to prevent drive-aways.

Fourth, and very importantly, you have a chance to discuss the joys of riding, and to mention little things that will cause the prospect to develop a loyalty to you and your store.

Obviously, it isn't always possible to go along on the ride. But it's also clear that when possible, it could be a great long-term benefit to business.

Whether or not you are able to ride with your customer, offering a test ride is a great way to make your trial close. If the customer doesn't wish to ride the bike, but you still think he is interested in this unit, you may wish to back up to the other approach, "Well, in any case, is this the kind of bicycle you had in mind?" Be careful not to get caught in the trap of selling the "trial close" instead of the bike. Some folks will not have the time, will be embarrassed, or be afraid of soiling their clothes. However, they are still interested in the bicycle.

Regardless of whether you use a trial close (and I highly recommend that you do), the final step in any sale is the CLOSE! If some salesmen fear that the customer will raise an objection, another whole bunch of 'em are afraid to hear "NO." Because of this fear, they are loathe to ask the question.

There is an easy answer to this dilemma. **Never ask a question that can be answered with a "No."** This advice is valuable from the beginning to the end of the sales dialogue, but it's particularly true of the close. The best close for a bicycle sale is the "choice" close. All you have to say is, "Would you like the lime green one with the dots or the magenta one with the tiger stripes?" (In the original "Principles of Bicycle Retailing" this question read, "Would you like the red one or the blue one?" How times change!)

The consumer has several choices for answers to this question. He may choose one of the two offered. He may ask about a third color. He may show some hesitation that would lead you to start asking questions again about his needs. But it is very hard to answer with a straight negative when you are offered a choice of two options.

There are many other "choices" you can use. Another very popular one is, "Will that be cash or charge?" How about, "We can have the bike ready in about five minutes. Do you prefer to take it with you or pick it up later?"

Another popular approach is called the assumption close. It is stronger than the choice close, and there are times when you may wish to use it.

You may have just tried the trial close, "Does this seem to be about what you had in mind?" The customer says, "Yes, I think so." You pull the bicycle around and point it in the direction of the cash register while saying, "O.K., what else can I get for you today." Better yet, as you will see in detail below, make a specific recommendation such as, "With this particular bicycle and the type of riding you'll be doing, let me recommend that you install some Mr. Tuffy's."

A very soft close is called the "YES" close. The idea of this one is to get the customer to say yes as many times as possible. Then the final yes is supposed to be a shoe-in. It is definitely effective, and almost like doing four trial closes before the real thing. A sample of how a "YES" close might sound would go like this:

You:       It seems that you definitely prefer the mountain bike.

Albert:    Yep. I really want to do some off-road riding.

You:       And the 18-speed with a grip shift is important to you?

Albert:    Yes indeed. I'll need all those gears up in the hills.

54

| You: | Do you like this candy apple paint job? |
| Albert: | You bet. It's really hot!! |
| You: | Let me have one of the guys fine tune it for you while we write it up. |

Any one of these closes and many others which you can read about in other books devoted to selling will work almost every time. The key thing to remember is that you *must close!*

People often need to be prodded into making a decision. This is especially true when the decision is one they are not used to making. One of your most important tasks as a salesman is to help them make a decision. You do this by listening carefully to their needs, making an enthusiastic presentation of the product that will answer these needs, and then helping them to a final decision with a gentle close.

My career in writing business books began because a good friend of mine who had recently purchased a successful bicycle dealership was having a tough time keeping the business going. He asked me for advice. Within an hour it became clear that his problem was lack of sales, not lack of opportunity. He guessed that only 50% of the people who entered his store with the express intent of purchasing a bicycle actually bought one.

When I explained that the number should be 90%, his reaction was disbelief. However, he agreed that 50% was too low. Over the next half hour or so, I trained him in only a single aspect of selling. I told him he must close every time. I only provided him with one closing method, "The red one or the blue one." Within days he called me, all excited: "Its amazing! It really works. I'm closing almost 90%."

Because of that meeting, I began to pay close attention to other dealers and clerks as they made presentations and sales. Very few knew how to sell. Even fewer ever made any attempt to close. Because of the need to help retailers learn to sell, *Principles of Bicycle Retailing* was written, and the first two editions have helped thousands to better sales.

If you don't pay attention to any other suggestion in this entire book, start closing every customer tomorrow. If you are an owner, make certain that each of your clerks is trained and coached in closing. Keep a chart on the wall that keeps track of the number of presentations that each salesperson makes and the number of sales completed as a percentage. Anyone who is falling under 90% needs a refresher course in selling. Suggest he read a book or listen to a tape on selling.

## FUNDAMENTAL NUMBER SIX - SELLING ADD-ONS

I am happy to report that after almost ten years of writing about the terrible margins bicycle dealers were willing to accept on the bike itself, these margins are on the increase. Based on the best statistical evidence available at this time, it would appear that most independent bicycle retailers are now averaging between 30-35% gross margin.

I wholeheartedly believe that this average will eventually settle in at 35%, and that the best shops will do even better. However, immutable laws of retailing make it clear that margins on clothing and accessories will always be greater than that on bicycles. In addition, if a cost accountant was to fully capture the overhead that should be charged to the bicycle as compared to that which should be charged to the accessories, the profit variable on accessories would be even more favorable.

Nothing in that last paragraph should suggest that you stop selling bicycles and sell only aftermarket products. I did suggest something of the sort in *Principles of BIcycle Retailing's* second edition, and there were a few shops who tried this approach with some success. With the recent improvement in margins, I withdraw that recommendation.

That said, you want to be certain that you meet all of your customer's needs at the time of a bicycle purchase, not merely the vehicle itself. It is important to the financial success of your business, as well as to the benefit of the customer, to be certain that he has everything needed to enjoy his new bike to the fullest.

Some salespeople become worried after writing up $400, $500, $600 or more for the two-wheeler, the customer will be "tapped out," in shock, sales resistant, or just plain ready to leave. Allow me to provide you with several good reasons why you should bury this fear, and keep on selling:

1.  To the extent that you allow your new customer to leave without a lock, and the bicycle is stolen before he purchases one, whom do you suppose he will blame? This could just as easily apply to many other accessories that if the customer begins using his purchase without them, he could be inconvenienced, or injured. Examples would include tire liners to avoid the inconvenience of a flat or a helmet to avoid potential injury.

2.  If you don't provide recommendations for accessories, your customer is very likely to ask riding companions for ideas on where to purchase items that they are using. This could mean that all your hard work to develop a customer could be lost when he goes somewhere else for clothes, a computer, or a water bottle and cage.

3.  It is much easier to develop the presentation for your customer's other needs while his usage is still fresh on your mind. It should be quite easy for you to plug in the appropriate tools, upgrades, and accessories at the time of the sale. If the new rider is truly out of cash, he'll let you know, and you can offer him some alternatives for getting the items as quickly as possible. (It makes just as much sense to put these kinds of items on layaway as it does the bike.)

Therefore, after you have closed the sale of the bicycle, you will want to pause only a few seconds before making a comment such as: "With the type of riding you'll to be doing, I would recommend a guaranteed U-lock, a helmet, and some gloves. Here is the kind of lock most of our customers use."

This approach allows for a continuation of the positive atmosphere you have achieved by using the professional sales approach described above. I'm sure that you can recall situations where a salesperson has earned your complete confidence and you were eager for him to help you through the purchase of products you were unfamiliar with.

After selling the individual three or four of the most important accessories, you may wish to broaden your approach, and ease off a bit. You might say, "Would you like to look at any clothes, night riding gear, or touring bags?" This gives the customer a chance to point you in the best direction for the balance of the sale. He may also take this opportunity to indicate he is ready to stop for now.

Finally, here is a fun selling tip that might add $5 or so worth of high margin accessories to every bicycle sale. This technique was best demonstrated in the Columbo TV mystery movies. After Columbo would finish interrogating a suspect or witness, he would say good-bye and leave. Just as he was about to close the door, he would step back in and casually say, "Oh. Just one more thing." This approach is designed to allow the witness to relax and let down defenses, in the hope that the "one last question" will catch him off guard.

The sales variation of this technique is not designed to catch your customer off guard, but it does borrow from the Columbo approach in that the customer will tend to relax as you write-up or key-in the sale. While you are doing so, you casually suggest, "Oh! You'll surely need a water bottle." (There are other inexpensive accessory items that you could use for this final add-on.) At least 90% of the time, the customer will say, "O.K. Throw one in." If you should use a water bottle for this idea, you could stretch your benefit even further by using one with you store name printed on it.

## CRITICALLY IMPORTANT INFORMATION

You have just finished reading a short study on the basics of selling. A small percentage of you have realized that if you were to take this material to heart and apply it starting tomorrow, it could very likely change the entire direction of your life.

Most of the rest of you sped through this section because: 1. You have a better way to sell; 2. You don't like to sell, and don't want to deal with a method for improvement in this skill; 3. You've read other sales methods similar to this, ignored them, and you feel you're doing just fine.

The reason I know that these thoughts are coursing through your mind is that I have shared those counterproductive ideas in the past. In my case, the situation was compounded by the fact that I had been selling since I was five years old, and I held two University degrees. How could anyone possibly teach ME anything about selling?

It wasn't until I was about 25 years old that I read *Think and Grow Rich* by Napolean Hill. I had read at least half a dozen other "how to sell" books, but somehow this one either told the story a little differently, or I was at an age where I was better able to listen to the voice of wisdom. In any case, I paid very careful attention to the methods suggested by Hill, and my selling career jumped into high gear.

Please, don't pass up this opportunity to increase your selling power, your earning potential, and your personal self esteem. You can accomplish all three by applying the above six very simple principles to your current occupation.

**GO BACK!!! READ THIS SECTION AGAIN!! MAKE YOURSELF A PLEDGE TO USE AT LEAST ONE OF THESE TECHNIQUES STARTING TOMORROW. AS YOU MASTER ONE OR TWO, COME BACK TO THIS MATERIAL AND READ IT AGAIN. THEN INCORPORATE ANOTHER ONE OR TWO OF THESE FUNDAMENTALS INTO YOUR DAILY SELLING APPROACH.**

*The appendix of this book will list several excellent selling books and other aids. However, the interesting thing about all the great salesmen who have written books on how to sell is that they all have the same message: Be enthusiastic, find the need, handle objections with questions, shut up, and close. They will use different headings, anecdotes, and teaching methods, but the basic five fundamentals will always be there.*

"Mr. Jones Says He Isn't In??"

# CHAPTER 5

# ADVANCED SALES
# TECHNIQUES

In most of life's pursuits, much success can be had by continually practicing the fundamentals. With consistent practice, many actions become like second nature. When this occurs, it becomes easier to use this base of knowledge, discipline, and success to reach even greater levels of expertise.

Riding a bicycle certainly represents an example of the above. Almost any five year old can learn, within an hour or so, to balance a two-wheeler and steer it on a straight course. With a reasonable amount of practice in fundamentals like proper body positioning, good pedal-stroking techniques, and handling, even the least athletic will soon be able to ride with the pack, or keep up on the hills.

Once these fundamental skills become second nature, the rider can begin to think about following a better line, reduce whipping, or determine when to draft and when to break away.

Likewise in selling. The techniques that follow are better learned after the fundamentals are solidly in place. You can reach 80% to 90% effectiveness with good fundamentals alone. This may be enough for many people. However, for those of you who are interested in becoming top sales producers, first work diligently on the ideas in Chapter 4. When you feel that you have totally incorporated them into your sales methodology, the advanced selling concepts in the next several pages will start you on your way to championship high-caliber results.

# THE REAL MEANING OF CUSTOMER SERVICE

It took me awhile to wake up to this idea. I thought what I had done my entire professional career was customer service. However, the concept has been re-defined for the '90s.

Part of the change has to do with the fact that the American consumer is being totally spoiled. The choices available on how to spend one's hard-earned discretionary dollars are many times what they were only a decade ago. Even the variety of brands within each category is exploding in number.

The consumer is bombarded by advertising from every direction. Consumers can't escape the constant sales effort. Innovative promoters are even trying to take their message into the stalls of public restrooms. It is becoming harder and harder to get the bike shop's message heard through all of the noise.

The number and variety of outlets for consumer products keep expanding. Thirty years ago in the bicycle industry, a bicycle could be purchased from an independent bike dealer or a department store like Sears. Then came discounters, mail order, warehouse clubs, catalog stores, home shopping networks, and we are now beginning to see the advent of bicycle shop franchising and mega-chains.

Expanding product varieties and sales outlets have caused the consumer to become more demanding. The consumer now says, "If I can't get what I want for the price I want, when I want, from you, I have many other choices. And if no one can give me the kind of bicycle I want, I'll try running, skiing, swimming, or aerobics on my VCR."

Many business writers believe that we are experiencing "the end of the mass market." It used to be that the manufacturer conceived of a product and tried to advertise it into popularity. Today, the manufacturer has to listen carefully to the entire line of distribution to determine what consumers want. Then, he must be ready to turn on a dime when the fickle consumer has a change of heart.

Thus too, in the bike shop. Less than a generation ago there were only ten speeds, three speeds, 20" bikes, and juvenile. Today, the available variations fill an annual issue of *Bicycling*. Some shops are reacting to this situation by carrying only a few lines in depth. Others are trying to maintain stock of seven, ten, or even more brands. The situation is similar for clothing, helmets, and major accessory categories.

As a seller of product and service, your success in the '90s will be largely tied to how well you listen to what your customer is saying. The more sophisticated you are in determining what cyclists in your community need and want, the easier it will be for you to build your business into a powerhouse. Consumers are willing to pay extra for that kind of special service, and they will tell their friends about the difference.

Therefore, your job as owner, seller, and sales manager of a bike store is to ensure that you and your sales staff are listening to your customers in a general sense, and also that you pay special attention to the concept of "Find the Need and Fill It" from Chapter 4. Once you are confident of what your customer needs, you can then communicate to them that you can fill this need.

You do this specifically with the sales presentation that spells out features and benefits that will solve problems for that individual consumer. You also communicate your ability to solve problems for all consumers you hope to reach through advertising, promotion, window display, store layout, and in-store signage and promotion.

## THE FEAR FACTOR

Show me someone who has sold for a living, and I'll show you someone who has had to deal with certain fears and anxieties. I will touch on some of these briefly, then direct you to other resources where the most common sales fears are dealt with more thoroughly.

**Fear of "NO."** - It is the rare individual who isn't somewhat affected by the rejection implied in a "NO." Many salespeople are quick to conclude that the customer said "no" because either the presentation was not good enough, they were not good enough, or the customer just didn't like them.

After tasting rejection on any given day, it becomes harder to approach the next selling opportunity with the same enthusiasm (if at all). There are several solutions to this set of feelings. However, as in any situation where a person is dealing with overcoming negative feelings, the cure is not instant. The salesperson suffering from fear of rejection will need to take these "pills" every four to six hours until symptoms cease.

1. There will be times that you fail to communicate the sales message properly, or adequately understand the need. However, it will be only the rarest situation where you will not be able to quickly recognize your error. Often, this will even take place before the customer is out of the store.

   When you do lose the customer, however, and can clearly see your mistake, don't beat yourself up over it. Success is made up of a series of failures. We learn to stand by finding out first how not to fall down. Each sales failure will bring you closer to excellence.

2. Have you ever met someone and instantly disliked him? Maybe he reminds you of someone in your past who you didn't like. It isn't his fault, but you have a prejudice against him before he even opens his mouth.

   Once in a great while, a consumer may feel the same about you. You may sense this, and if you lose the sale, may chalk up the lost sale to being unlovable. Again, this doesn't mean there is anything wrong with you. The problem was with the customer. You will not be liked by everyone, so be encouraged by the many who appreciate you, and not discouraged by the few who are too blind to see how lovable you are.

3. Occasionally you'll ring up a big NO SALE after a perfect presentation where you felt as if the customer was ready to suggest a lifelong friendship. This can result in hours of second guessing. What did you do wrong? Maybe it was my breath? Did I come on too strong?

   One explanation for not making a sale may be the strange phenomenon that sometimes makes it difficult for some people to buy from someone they like. There are other situations where the customer may not have had the money or budget for the bike, and was too embarrassed to tell you. The list of possibilities is endless as to why a sale may be lost, and most of them have nothing to do with you, your charm, or your ability.

4.  Plan for "NO's." Figure you will get about 10%. If you get a lot more than 10%, just study Chapter 4 again. Pay special attention to the section on closing.

    If you recognize that you are going to get a certain percentage of customers who don't buy what you're selling, you can replace the fear of rejection with an understanding of the fact that each "no" gets you that much closer to a "yes." In fact, if you have a 90% closing ratio, each "no" should mean that the next nine will be "yes."

5.  Finally. . . If you have followed the selling method outlined in Chapter 4, and you truly believe that you have presented a bicycle or accessory that is appropriate to the need of the customer, but you don't get the sale, don't blame yourself. The customer is the one who made the mistake. After all, customers are only human and quite capable of error.

**Fear of the Initial Approach** - In a retail setting, it is very common for a salesperson to be timid about starting the conversation with a new customer. The thoughts racing through his head might include: "He looks like he wants to be left alone," or, "If I approach her, she'll think I'm too aggressive," or, "I'll give him some time," or, "I can already tell. He's not going to like me."

Please go back and read the suggested opening lines in Chapter 4 under "Be Enthusiastic." If you approach the customer with an enthusiastic attitude and any line other than, "May I help you," I assure you that 90% will be friendly and responsive. (10% of the population is grouchy all the time.)

Once you have seen how nicely people respond to this type of introduction, your fear of the initial approach will go away.

**Fear of Success** - Strange, but true, is the fact that one of the toughest fears for many in business and/or sales to overcome is the fear of success. There is almost a superstitious aspect to this. The salesperson who experiences these feelings believes that, were he to reach a high level of sales, he would not be able to sustain that level because he would have gotten there by luck, not skill. Because he can't stand the idea of becoming successful, just to then fall back to an average level again, he prefers to stay in the average range from the onset.

It is a tremendous waste of time and energy to worry about the future. There are only three possible outcomes of any future event that someone could be worried about.

First, there could be a positive result, and therefore the worry was unfounded. Second, there was no result at all because situations changed so much that the event didn't happen. Again, the worry was to no avail. Third, the expected negative result occurs, but worrying about it didn't keep it from happening, and very probably made it worse.

Worry is also deleterious to your physical and emotional health. The wasted effort devoted to the business of worrying may very well create more calamity than the worst possible outcome of the event being worried about.

For a salesperson, worry is the enemy of enthusiasm. Therefore, when the worry is concentrated on maintaining sales levels, the very act of worrying will negatively impact sales. The result is a self-fulfilling prophecy.

Worry is not to be confused with "concern." Concern creates action designed to avert potential negatives. You should be concerned when traffic is slow in the store, and act immediately to do something to stimulate traffic. However, worry will not change the situation one way or the other.

## MOTIVATING YOURSELF

PMA (positive mental attitude) was the sales buzzword of the '70s, and only the American need for new slogans could possibly explain why it is not still in vogue. If I were to list the behaviors that I believe contribute most to life success, they would be:

1. Belief in God or following spiritual guidance.

2. Writing down believable goals.

3.  Maintaining a positive mental attitude.

4.  Having a servant's heart.

5.  Constantly educating yourself.

Today there are those who believe only in themselves. They are, however, unlikely to be able to sustain this idea forever. Everyone will have a string of mistakes (slump, bad luck, bad timing) that can bring into question belief in self. However, belief in spirituality as a personal sustainer of good for your life makes it possible to maintain a consistent attitude that your actions will have long term rewards . . . even in the face of catastrophe.

The opposite approach can be seen in the individual who believes that no matter what they do, they are at the mercy of other persons, or events, that are able to control their will. These individuals will commonly use words such as "go with the flow." They will spend countless hours evaluating how their life has been shaped by their genetics, their parents, or their schools. These are the same folks who will look at the successful individuals around them and pronounce them "lucky."

Therefore, the first step in personal motivation is to adopt a mind set that says: **"I am in control of my destiny. No one else can alter this without my permission. I can choose to fly with the eagles, swim with the sharks, or lie around with the sloths. I make my own happiness. It is a good idea for me to seek out spirituality and others who can fill my needs, but if I rely on other people to make me happy, I can expect disappointment. I will refrain from offering excuses for those parts of my life that are not as I would like. I will replace that thinking with immediate movement to institute those actions that I believe will gain the ends I seek."**

Number Two is covered in detail in Chapter 2. In addition, there are several books suggested in the appendix that will further enlighten you on the benefits and methods of setting goals.

The best way to maintain a positive mental attitude is to practice the other four items on the list. In addition, if you were not endowed with an optimistic outlook, you may need to make a decision. It may be the hardest decision you ever had to carry out. Pessimism and negativism are as addicting as the most powerful drug. They do create certain chemicals in your system that you become dependent upon. In addition, they are psychologically addicting.

A negative approach to life allows for excuse making, blaming, and rationalizing. If you can always blame your shortcomings on something or somebody else, you have no accountability or responsibility. It's obvious that life is easier when you don't have to worry about those two things ruining your party.

Life may be easier under those conditions, but certainly not fulfilling or enjoyable. Recognizing your responsibility for your actions and sometimes even the actions of others creates activity, improves self-esteem, overcomes pessimism and develops character.

One pessimist told me that he didn't want to get his hopes up only to have them dashed. By expecting nothing, or the worst, he never was disappointed and often pleasantly surprised. In looking at his life, he seems to be the only one that isn't disappointed with the results and the pleasant surprises have been few and far between.

To have a positive mental attitude, it isn't necessary to believe there's a pot of gold at the end of every rainbow. I know plenty of optimistic people that have their feet firmly planted on the ground. However, they do expect the best of people and of life. They get disappointed, but it doesn't last. They have setbacks, like anyone else, but they jump right back in the saddle and start chasing the next opportunity.

It would take a very long book to discuss the methods for changing an attitude of negativism into PMA. Fortunately, there have been several excellent ones already written. *See You at the Top* by Zig Zigler and *The Power of Positive Thinking* by Norman Vincent Peale come immediately to mind.

Number Four, "Having a Servant's Heart," has to do with one of the fundamental principles of leadership. For instance, the American system of government is based upon the idea of the leaders serving the people, not the other way around. (Surely, we could all argue that reality doesn't always equal intent.)

To the extent that our elected leaders were to act in the way intended, they would be substantially more effective as their constituency would recognize their forthright intentions immediately.

This premise is true for everyone who leads others. As the owner of a retail business, your employees will also have dramatically more respect for you if they sense you are acting on the basis of their needs, not your own. Your customers, likewise, will appreciate the attitude that comes with such an approach to life.

Finally, the person who constantly educates him or herself will never be in a position of being obsolete. The world is changing very rapidly. It took a large room to house a computer in 1955 that wouldn't fill a watch case today, and tomorrow may be the size of a molecule. Read everything you can find on subjects that will affect your life's success. Attend classes that will stretch you and open up new opportunities in your future.

## SALES MANAGEMENT

It never ceases to amaze me that many otherwise intelligent and well- trained sales people put up tremendous resistance to the idea of setting goals. The store owner or sales manager will often have to be threatened by dire consequences before digging out these projections. Even more amazing is the absolute fact that many owners do not set overall sales goals for the store, for sub-categories of products and services within the store, or for their own personal sales production.

My amazement doesn't stem from a lack of understanding the reasons for such reluctance. Here are just a few of the reasons why owners, managers, and sales clerks resist setting goals:

1.  Incorrect belief that goals are unproductive, unnecessary, or beneath the dignity of the individual in question.

2.  Fear of falling short of goals. You can't fail to reach a goal you haven't set.

3.  Concern that whatever goal is selected, the manager will add to that number for purposes of future evaluations or bonus programs.

4.  Lack of confidence in ability to predict the future. This commonly stems from a perfectionist attitude. You know this problem exists when the individual can't produce projections without stacks of historical data.

I have never seen a consistently top producer who did not constantly set goals for himself. However, I have seen numerous examples of potentially brilliant salesmen who have not had goals, and they come up short of their potential repeatedly.

The most successful individuals set goals for every part of their life: professional, educational, relational, physical, and spiritual. They set long-term (twenty years or longer), medium-term (one to twenty years), and monthly/daily/hourly goals as the situation warrants. These movers and shakers set out a course to a worthwhile destination, and then make a plan to follow that course.

In setting sales goals for your store, or in evaluating the goals set by your sales staff, take the following into consideration:

1.  The goal amounts must be believed to be achievable. There is no faster way to cause a salesperson to become dispirited than to establish a goal that is beyond his ability to comprehend its successful attainment.

2.  On the other hand, the goal must be challenging. Good salespeople love a challenge. Of course, if you have established a commission or bonus program to go along with reaching a certain sales figure, the adrenaline pumps even more.

3.  The number you set must be high enough to be profitable. If the highest, believable expectation is below profitability, you should get out of the business.

4.  It is acceptable to change major life goals when it becomes apparent that you no longer have the burning desire necessary to achieve one or more of these. Generally, the most successful people will replace these dropped aspirations with a new dream.

You should, however, be very careful about changing sales goals, unless it is to increase them. If you begin to cave in to the unmet daily and weekly numbers, and bow to the pressure to lower your monthly and annual goals, you may develop a very bad habit. Once you start lowering expectations, it is easy to do so again and again.

The better approach is to examine the reasons for the lower-than-expected numbers in the prior periods to determine if the reason was correctable. It is my opinion that unless the goals were totally unrealistic, the sales plan can be gotten back on track . . . assuming the **burning desire** is present.

4.  Keep a visible daily record. Goals, of course, are not merely for the sales department. For example, the bottle manufacturing employees at AC International had been averaging about 1,800 bottles per shift at one point. We put up a chalkboard that showed each day of the week, each machine, and each shift. The first week we tried this, the chart looked something like this.

|  | Monday | Tuesday | Wednesday | Thursday | Friday |
|---|---|---|---|---|---|
| **First Shift** | | | | | |
| **Small bottles** | 1000 | 1100 | 1200 | 1300 | 1275 |
| **Large bottles** | 900 | 1050 | 1101 | 1200 | 1200 |
| | | | | | |
| **Second Shift** | | | | | |
| **Small bottles** | 1050 | 1100 | 1200 | 1300 | 1325 |
| **Large bottles** | 1000 | 1100 | 1102 | 1150 | 1150 |
| | | | | | |
| **Third Shift** | | | | | |
| **Small bottles** | 1075 | 1150 | 1250 | 1250 | 1300 |
| **Large bottles** | 1050 | 1100 | 1100 | 1150 | 1200 |
| | | | | | |
| **TOTAL** | 6075 | 6600 | 6953 | 7350 | 7450 |

By the end of the first week, we had optimized the capacity of the equipment and increased production by over 40%. (First shift Monday compared with average shift on Friday.) We never said there was a competition. We never indicated what we believed the optimum number of bottles per shift was. We just put up a scoreboard.

You could try the same approach with such headings as "bicycles sold," "helmets sold," or "total sales volume." These could be shown by day/by salesperson.

5. Establish rewards for achieving goals. This is true for yourself and for your staff. It is especially necessary for those who have not had experience with setting and reaching goals.

Start with yourself. How can you reward yourself for accomplishing certain sales levels? What would really motivate you? A day off? A date with your spouse at a favorite restaurant? A weekend in the mountains? When you have arrived at the answer, think about the things you might do differently with your time and energy during the next five days if the result would be that reward.

If you haven't been able to quite visualize this concept, consider this: What ideas for selling more bikes could you come up with if I offered to send you on a two-week, all-expense-paid trip to Hawaii if you could sell 50% more bicycles next week than you did this week? Would you stand out in the middle of the street and drag people in? Would you start calling friends and relatives to see if they, or someone they know, might need a bike?

With that illustration in mind, you should be able to design a personal reward system that makes sense. After you do this, you may want to do the same approach for each salesperson. In fact, you may want to develop some type of bonus for every employee based on a performance criterion.

The more intelligent and successful a person is, the more likely he will be to believe that he will not be motivated by an incentive program. He will point very quickly to his record of success and assure you that he already does everything he knows how to do to maximize his sales.

The reality is quite the opposite. Assuming that he is either motivated by the bonus offered, or that he is the type of individual who needs to win, he will produce more when he has an incentive. I have proven this repeatedly with every type of employee.

## KEEPING TRACK

I would suggest that you put up a chart in the back room or break area that would create some competition between members of your sales staff. It will also allow you to garner much needed information about your staff and your profitability.

| Salesman | MON | TUE | WED | THU | FRI | SAT | TOTAL | AVG PER HOURS | CLOSE RATIO |
|---|---|---|---|---|---|---|---|---|---|
| **Linda** | | | | | | | | | |
| hours worked | 4 | 8 | 6 | 8 | 4 | 8 | **38** | | |
| presentations | IIII | III | III | IIIII | III | IIIIIII | **25** | 0.66 | |
| units sold | II | II | III | III | II | IIIII | **17** | 0.45 | 68% |
| dollars sold | 125 | 920 | 1950 | 1200 | 975 | 2800 | **8970** | 236 | |
| **Dave** | | | | | | | | | |
| hours worked | 8 | 8 | 8 | 0 | 8 | 8 | **40** | | |
| presentations | IIIIIII | IIII | IIII | | IIIIII | IIIIIIII | **29** | 0.73 | |
| units sold | IIIII | II | IIII | | IIII | IIIIII | **21** | 0.53 | 72% |
| dollars sold | 2200 | 1050 | 1400 | | 2020 | 2650 | **9320** | 233 | |
| **Sandi** | | | | | | | | | |
| hours worked | 0 | 8 | 8 | 8 | 8 | 8 | **40** | | |
| presentations | | III | IIIII | IIII | IIIIII | IIIII | **23** | 0.58 | |
| units sold | | II | II | II | III | III | **12** | 0.3 | 52% |
| dollars sold | | 580 | 975 | 1020 | 1440 | 1140 | **5155** | 128 | |
| **Jerry** | | | | | | | | | |
| hours worked | 4 | 0 | 4 | 4 | 4 | 8 | **24** | | |
| presentations | II | | II | III | III | IIIIIIII | **18** | 0.75 | |
| units sold | II | | II | II | III | IIIIIII | **16** | 0.67 | 89% |
| dollars sold | 775 | | 1075 | 1250 | 1150 | 3215 | **7465** | 311 | |

I would hope that the possibilities of such a chart jump off the page at you. At least for this week, one of your people well underperformed the others. You also had one star, and he had the least hours. Linda had a poorer closing ratio but more dollar volume than Dave. With this information in hand, and assuming they are not one week aberrations, you can begin to make some decisions about training, motivation, hours, and even termination.

Some stores are already able to gather this data through their computer systems. However, be sure to take the second step of posting the results where all sales personnel can see who's doing what. When we started the bottle program at AC International, we saw those excellent results presented above. After a few months, the lead men became lax about posting the results even though the daily numbers were still given to the inventory control department.

If you speculated that the numbers went down again, you were correct. The impact is far greater when every employee in the shop can see how every other employee is doing.

"Things Are A Bit Out of Whack Today,
We've Gotten Calls From
3 Customers and 9 Suppliers."

# CHAPTER 6

# TWENTY FIVE WAYS
# TO SELL MORE - TOMORROW

What did your sales totals look like in 1991? Were they up or down from 1990? How did 1990 compare with 1989? If you were like most shops in the USA during that period, you probably weren't too happy about the results. "But," you rationalize, "those were recessionary years. Recession means less sales, right?"

There can be no doubt that recessions bring lower sales. That, after all, is built into the definition of recession. HOWEVER, it only means less total sales of goods and services throughout the economy. Many, many individual industries and businesses enjoyed substantial increases in the 1991 recession, and in every other recession. This chapter is dedicated to the proposition that it is **totally** a function of the management of any business whether sales go up or down. How far up or down will be effected by many external forces, including local and national economic conditions. However, it is important enough to restate - **THE MANAGEMENT OF ANY ENTERPRISE IS 100% RESPONSIBLE FOR THE SALES RESULTS OF THAT SPECIFIC BUSINESS.**

Let's put a little meat on those bones. When the economy is moving along at a good pace, it doesn't take a business genius to increase sales year after year. One might compare such a situation to a fish living in a hatchery. There is generally a great deal of competition, but there is also an abundance of prospects for keeping well fed.

Take that same fish, and put it in the wild. The prospects are much harder to find, and they are probably not as meaty. This is similar to the recessionary situation in a bike shop. Consumers are harder to find, and their wallets aren't as fat. The key to survival for the fish and the bike shop is to dramatically increase the effort to find prospects. Having found a "live one" (customer) the need to maximize the opportunity with that prospect is especially important.

Unfortunately for many business people, the onset of tough economic times actually results in no additional effort in hunting and gathering. Even more curiously, there is often a decline in both of these areas.

In my book, *Bicycle Dealer's Guide to Getting Rich in the Recession*, I detail a strategy for preparing your enterprise for recession, maximizing sales and profits during any such economic slowdown, and increasing opportunities for wealth-building that are unique to such periods. The optimum time to read that book is not six months into a recession, but well before the next one.

It is a certainty that the USA will enter into another recession. I predict that this will occur in about 1998. It will be due, in part, to the emotional unease of a millennium change. It will also be due to the fact that economies need to ring out excesses from time to time, and generally, these adjustments occur six or so years apart.

The proactive ideas that follow do not require a recession to be valid. They are beneficial during any soft sales period, whether these be weather related, seasonal, or just a lull during a strong season.

**Get on the phone** - Call your best customers. Ask them about their family, their job, and, naturally, their riding. Keep a card on each of these customers that details the names of family members, the nature of the employment, and their riding activities.

After the small talk, tell them about some new product that they might find beneficial. You might offer them a special price on an item they have considered purchasing. How about a service special now available because of your service department being slow at this time?

Ask if they have any friends that might be interested in getting a bicycle. If you have the right type of rapport with this particular client, suggest some benefit (such as cash or products) that you might pay for each new customer he sends in. (To learn from the master of this approach, read *How to Sell Anything to Anybody* by Joe Girard.)

**Get in the mail** - Develop several mailing lists. If you don't have a computer, an investment in even the least sophisticated computer and printer will give you the ability to compile a mailing list and label-making capacity. It will also allow you to develop and print simple letters, brochures, or newsletters to keep your customers informed about what's going on in your bike shop.

Among the mailing lists you may wish to keep would be these:

1. Complete list of all customers who have ever been in the store
2. Those who purchased a bicycle
3. Those who spent more than $50 (Or pick another dollar amount)
4. Those who come into the store regularly (4, 8, 12-times per year)
5. Those who have filled out a form specifically asking for information on new bicycles, accessories, or other needs
6. Professionally prepared lists of those in your geographic area by age group, income class, or other criteria

Mailing to these various groups is something you should be doing at all times, but it is especially important to reach out to them when you are slow. With the mail/merge capabilities of most word processing programs, you can develop very personal sounding letters that would accomplish by mail much of what was recommended in "Get on the phone" above. This type of mailing should be sent on company letterhead. Here's an example.

# SPOKEN FAR BIKE SHOP

Billy Smith
333 Arrow Drive
E. Northtown, SD 55555

Dear Billy:

I was checking in some new products the other day, and it occurred to me that some of them might be interesting to you. We have several new items that are especially useful for *mountain bikes*.

We're having a special sale right now for friends of SPOKEN FAR. If you come in during the month of October, I'll give you a 15% discount on any accessories you want. We can also do a Winter Prep on your bike for only $15.00, and we can do it while you wait.

By the way, *Billy*, if any of your friends are interested in buying a bike, now is a very good time. Tell them I will give them a very special deal if they mention your name.

We appreciate having you as a customer and look forward to your next visit. Hope all is well with you.

Sincerely,

*John Winner*

John Winner
Owner

In this example, the items in *italics* would be specific for each letter. The rest of the letter would be generic.

A simple newsletter can talk of personal matters (like Bill Quinn does so well in "Partly Personal"), upcoming rides and events, new products, and/or sales and specials. The more professionally prepared the better, but it doesn't have to be a Madison Avenue masterpiece to result in bringing some "live ones" into the store. If you can't write at all, contact your local community college or university. A journalism student might help you with this effort for a few dollars or for extra class credit.

Consider the following sample:

# THE WHEEL NEWS

## EVENT NEWS

Every Saturday morning at 7:00 a.m. a group of riders meet here at the store and take a two hour ride together. We generally divide into two groups. Some like to move a little faster. Some a little slower. Both groups have a great time. After the ride, we supply the refreshments. No need to reserve. Just show up.

## BUYING GOOF

Somebody wasn't paying attention and we double-ordered our lycra spandex helmet covers. Now we have a whole bunch. Help us move 'em out and we'll help you save some money. Regular $5.99. Now $4.40

## HOTTEST NEW PRODUCT

We've just received a new water bottle that comes with a freezable core in the middle. All you do is stick it in your freezer and in a couple of hours it's frozen. Then just pour your refreshment in and you're ready to go. Won't dilute your drink. No need for ice cubes. It's called the Prem Cool Bottle, and it sells for only $6.95.

### BICYCLE PRICES NOT KEEPING UP WITH INFLATION

Did you know that if bicycle prices had risen over the past 40 years at the same rate as many other items, a basic starter unit would be about $300? For a pretty good bike shop two-wheeler, you'd be paying $1,000 or more. And for top of the line wheels you'd have to shell out $5,000 or more.

Just check out some of the prices from 1952 compared to today. Then look at the bike prices.

| • • • • • • | 1952 | 1992 | % Increase |
|---|---|---|---|
| Mail a letter | $ .03 | $ .29 | 867% |
| Gallon of gas | .18 | 1.08 | 500% |
| Movie ticket | .25 | 7.50 | 2900% |
| Cola in machine (8 oz) | .05 | .50 | 900% |
| Lowest price car | 500.00 | 5000.00 | 900% |
| Greeting card | .05 | .75 | 1400% |
| Starter bike (dept store) | 30.00 | $75.00 | 150% |
| Adult bike (bike store) | 100.00 | 200.00 | 100% |

I would prepare a newsletter like the above on 8 1/2" X 11" or legal 8 1/2" x 14" paper. Maybe you could put it on a distinctively colored paper. Come up with a distinctive masthead. Now fold, staple, affix address labels, and mail. To mail 1,000 of these per month would probably take you six man hours and cost $400 tops, with first-class postage. To save money, get a bulk rate permit, and print the number right on the newsletter.

Other mailing possibilities include:

1. Post cards with a special, or to announce a one day sale

2. Co-op catalog - Call Catalyst or another progressive supplier offering such a service.

3. Top of the line professional mass mailing - Look in phone book for mailing companies.

4. Birthday cards

5. Reminder to come in for free, new bike adjustments.

**Get on the phone ... Part Two -** There are many, many people, organizations, and companies in your town that will not necessarily come looking for you when it is time to buy a bike. You can put those off hours, days, or weeks to good use calling prospects such as the following:

1. The police department. There is a major movement nationally to put cops on bikes. It has been very successfully done in hundreds of communities as of this writing. If your city hasn't tried it yet, suggest it to the chief of police or to the city council at its next meeting. If they are already in the program, you want to sell them product and offer them service.

2. Municipal, county, regional, and state government. Many government agencies can or could use bicycles. This is most common where there are large physical plants, parks, beaches, and other large areas requiring security or delivery of messages or parts.

3. Corporations. Similar to government, there are many companies that currently have bicycle fleets or who could benefit from using bikes. The best candidates are those with large physical

plants or those who are spread out with several buildings around town.

4.  Health Clubs, YMCA's, other community fitness organizations and Corporations with fitness facilities. All of these and more purchase exercise bicycles and equipment. They also need a source for repairing that equipment. In addition, when you supply your exercise products to them (with your store name clearly emblazoned on them), you are likely to have referral business as a result. I know of one dealer who used to sell 1,000 exercycles a year at $400 each using this approach. He retired at age forty.

5.  Day care centers, nurseries, and kindergartens. As with health clubs, sell and service juvenile items with the real goal of advertising to the kids' parents. A four-year-old who is riding a 16-inch bike at his pre-school is going to want one just like it for home. If it has a big sticker on it with your name and phone number, you are likely to get the business.

6.  Hotels and recreation areas. Selling and repairing rental bikes is a much better business than renting the bikes. (e.g. You don't have the liability problem.) There are probably two dozen businesses in your area who you could offer a service of bicycle rentals to and profit from rentals.

7.  Group sales. Take a note from the pages of other retailers and service providers. Why not offer special discounts and service deals to members of groups such as: Employees of large corporations, members of senior citizen groups, honor roll students, auto club members, police officers, public employees.

8.  Premium sales. You can make money selling imprinted bicycle items. Haven't you been approached by a salesman to put your store name on pencils, pens, calendars, and mugs for give-aways? Turn the table. Call on local banks, service clubs, pizza parlors, health clubs and movie theaters with an offer for them to purchase and give away bicycle water bottles, cycling caps, or other imprinted items.

For instance, an average commercial customer might buy 500 water bottles. You can buy these for around $1 each, and sell them easily for $2. This gives you a $1,000 sale at 50% margins. Is there anything else in your store that can bring those kinds of results?

9. Assembly and repair services. You may not care too much for the various department stores in your area that sell bicycles. They are the bad guys, right? Why not turn them into your best customer? Most do not do their own assembly of new bikes. They also need someone to fix bikes that are brought in with warranty problems. This can be a very profitable business and will not affect how many bicycles they sell one way or the other. Department store clerks are notoriously uninformed about repair. Why not be their local expert for such lucrative repair work.

**Get in your car -** Many of the ideas presented above require that you not only make a phone call, but that you get in your car (or on your bike) and go visit the decision maker. Here are a few tips for making such calls:

1. Be totally prepared. Have all the necessary materials, prices, and samples that you need. Know in advance as much as you can about the customer's needs. Have a game plan in mind, but be prepared to give and take as you learn more.

2. Dress at least as well as you expect the buyer is dressed. This may mean you need to wear a suit and tie. It may mean only a dress shirt. It will rarely mean that you should go in your T-shirt or shop jacket. You want the buyer to believe that you are knowledgeable and successful.

3. Go over the selling chapter above. You will want to employ all the same techniques in this type of selling as you do with consumers in your store. Be enthusiastic, find the need and fill it, answer objections with questions, shut up, and **close**.

4. Be certain to take good notes. Then follow up if you didn't close the deal on the first call. In this selling situation, the buyer has

many other things on his mind. Call as often as you can without becoming a total pest. Be bold enough to ask the buyer when he will make a decision, or when you can call back.

5.  Once you have made the sale and delivery, call at least once per month to see how the product is doing, and to see if you can be of any more service.

There are numerous opportunities available for you to sell bicycles and fitness products to other businesses and organizations in your area.

**Get in the paper** - Free publicity in your local newspaper is far more valuable than paid advertising. If you are not a good writer, maybe your spouse, an older child, a student, or one of your employees could take on the public relations job.

The big dailys are not the only possible source of free publicity. Check out the weeklys, advertising sheets, local club and organization newsletters, large corporation in-house publications, college and high school newspapers, and computer bulletin boards.

You also might develop a talk that you could give for local service clubs. Most have a half hour of each meeting devoted to area businessmen and community leaders giving a short speech. Generally, they are hard-pressed to find a good speaker fifty-two weeks a year. Most communities also have networking clubs like Le Tip that can provide you with additional business leads and opportunities.

**Get in the car . . . Part Two** - When the going gets tough, the tough get going. It may seem like a hard way to bring in customers, but community bulletin boards can be one more resource for building traffic. Campus, supermarket, and laundromat boards get very high usage.

**Get in another business** - I don't mean leave the bicycle business, but you may be able to expand your product mix to include related lines that would increase your total sales without increasing your overhead. Here are some suggestions for accomplishing that:

First, you would want to consider expansion within the bicycle world. Do you now carry juvenile bikes and accessories, clothing, energy drinks, exercise equipment, professional frame-sets, bicycle books and videos, roof racks, or recumbents? Any one of these items could be an opportunity for new sales. Of course, you will want to consider clearly the cost/benefit and risk/reward equations before any such move.

Second, you could look at related areas. I'm not certain that there are any new ideas in this area. Some that have been done successfully include: ski's, in-line skates, locksmithing, lawnmowers, triathlon products, hobbies, and snowboards. In general, I do not suggest this unless you determine that the your market area will never support a bikes-only shop. The exceptions are the contra-seasonal ski shop in the colder climates and in-line skates. These combinations seem to be good money makers. Be wary, however, of the possibility of skates being the latest "fad" that could easily fade.

Get in a joint promotion - Where are your customers when they are not on bicycles? What are your potential customers buying instead of bicycles and related equipment? How can you join forces with another business or organization to help both companies improve traffic?

Let's try one example. If you have a family bicycle shop, I'll bet your customers spend a bunch of time at McDonald's. Sure, we would like to think otherwise, but guess what? Facts is facts.

McDonald's and other fast food franchisers are constantly looking for ways to promote, and they are expert at milking promotions for all they are worth. You should also know that these types of enterprises experience almost exactly the same economic curves that you do.

Set up an appointment to see the local franchisee. Suggest that you partner up on: A ride (They especially like rides tied into causes like MS or Ronald McDonald's Houses.), a drawing with one or more bicycles as prizes, or a water bottle (with both your names printed on) given free with a large Coke.

Other companies in town that are likely to do joint promotions include:

1.  Movie theater (drawings, discount tickets)

2.  Ski shop (cross couponing)

3.  Auto retailer (new bike and rack with every car)

4.  Newspaper (paper carrier contests, drawings)

5.  Radio stations (call in contests)

6.  Theme parks (drawings and contests)

7.  Almost anyone

**Get a life** - Join a church, civic group, political club, PTA, or service club. Join more than one. Get active. You will sell bicycles as a result of these associations. Use networking as you get involved and let your fellow members know you are **the** source for their bicycle needs.

Then join with other bicycle retailers in your area. Set up a club on your own or as part of the NBDA (National Bicycle Dealer's Association). Use this affiliation to provide opportunities for exchange of ideas, joint events and promotions, and for good plain fun and fellowship. You will all sell more bicycles as a result. Ask the members of CABDA (The Chicago Area Bicycle Dealer's Association). They've had great success as a group promoting rides, races, consumer shows, and other events.

Produce activities designed to promote bicycling - Rides, centuries, races, exhibitions, classes, tours, and/or clubs. You can't do it all, but you should do some of it. What better time to start something like this than when business is slow!

I hope this chapter has caused you to realize that there is plenty of opportunity for you to be in control of your destiny, regardless of which way the economic winds are blowing. It took me less than three hours on a Saturday afternoon (with my toddler son interrupting every ten minutes), to conceive of and write this entire section. Surely, the next time things are slow in your town, you could re-read this section in twenty minutes and make some detailed plans within hours that will increase traffic and therefore, sales.

Effective Advertising Targets Markets Carefully.

# CHAPTER 7

# THE MAGIC OF MARKETING

As a retailer, your business represents the last step in the distribution chain. By the time a product reaches your store it has been conceived, designed, developed, engineered, packaged, advertised, promoted, manufactured, distributed, shipped, and received. On the face of it, one would think the retailer's marketing opportunity would be rather minimal.

While there is little you can change about the product when it arrives at your store, you still have an opportunity to make all the difference in the success of that item. In fact, one major obstacle to the retailer's success is the amount of marketing needs he is faced with compared with the time and money available for that task.

Retailers are on the front line of interesting the consumer in the product. They are the ultimate representative for the various products they sell. A retailer must market his store, his industry, his specific lines, and his niche. He is faced with most of the same advertising and promotional opportunities as the manufacturer and wholesaler and many more besides.

How can the "mom and pop" store possibly do a good job of promoting all the items that reach its shelves? The answer is, it can't be done with the current methods.

When I first wrote *Principles of Bicycle Retailing*, I saw a retail environment that was twenty years behind the times. The good news is that in the past ten years the industry has raced to catch up. The bad news is that our industry is still ten years behind other similar retail businesses. This is not entirely the fault of the retailers, but it does have a great deal to do with dealers' reluctance to organize for greater efficiency.

The Chicago Area Bicycle Dealers Association (CABDA) has contributed mightily to the strength of dealers served by that organization. Where is the CABDA in California, New England, or Colorado? Independent retailers will either join together for effective marketing or fall separately under the combined assault of Wal Mart, Toys R Us, REI Co-op, Performance Bicycle Shops, and other mass marketers and chains that are even now being organized. The National Bicycle Dealer's Association (NBDA) has made significant in-roads with its new regional chapters, but much work remains to be done.

The major manufacturers, importers, and wholesalers should take note of this prediction. Maybe they feel that they will be nimble enough to move out of the independent retail scene and into the mass market without missing a step, but there is substantial evidence to the contrary. With the use of EDI (Electronic Data Interface) there will be less and less need for middle men as direct computer link-ups between supplier and customer reduce the need for the services provided by distributors. Mass marketers, who have always preferred to deal directly with manufacturers are moving ever more in that direction.

As if to confirm this trend away from the traditional distributor/dealer distribution system, each of the major importers and distributors in the USA is struggling to be profitable. This trend started before the 1991 recession, and is unlikely to abate afterwards. The BWDA (Bicycle Wholesale Distributors Association) has shown renewed strength. Whether through this organization or in some other way, the various industry powerhouses need to move quickly to encourage independent dealers to unite in their marketing effort. These same major suppliers should be prepared to back up these efforts with money and personnel.

I called three years ago for the industry to tax itself $1 per bicycle and mount a national advertising campaign, much like the California Raisins' effort. I suggested that this be tied to the coming recognition by America that its youth are in big trouble physically, socially, and psychologically. Bicycling could be seen as a clean and exciting sport that kids could turn to instead of dope, sex, and MTV. America still needs solutions. And the independent bicycle dealer is still losing market share. Perhaps both problems could be helped by a united marketing effort of all who make their living in the industry. **Who will take the lead?**

The one-store independent bicycle shop will be under tremendous pressure to survive if there is not an organized effort to save this type of business entity. If you own such a business, you will need to be especially diligent in management and marketing to make up for your competitive disadvantage to chains of three to thirty stores and the discounters.

The following marketing concepts will work for independents, small chains, and franchises. Many of these approaches would be more cost effective if entered into jointly with other dealers. However, most can be accomplished by the smallest shop.

## Who, What, Why, Where, When, and How (Much)?

The first step in approaching the subject of any advertising or promotional campaign is to determine what you want to accomplish. If you have created a business plan, you will be able to look at the plan to see where advertising can help to make the plan successful. If you don't have an overall plan, you should still put aside some time to establish your reason for advertising.

The most likely reason for the retailer to advertise is to build traffic. However, this is only a partial answer. It isn't that difficult to build traffic for your store. You could give away gold coins or even dollar bills and you would be amazed at how many folks would come visit.

What kind of traffic do you need or want? Upscale families interested in purchasing bikes for the kids? Students needing transportation? Enthusiasts needing the latest craze or to move up to the next level of equipment? Maybe you'd like to have some of each, and throw in a few more groups, too. The question is, "Who is in your target audience at this time, and what do you think they want?"

It is impossible to appeal to every type of rider at all times. Your financial and personnel resources would be strained beyond hope. You may be able to advertise to more than one group at a time. You may even be able to communicate more than one idea or solution at a time. However, the more focused you are, the more likely you are to get results.

Here are a few examples of "focused" reasons for advertising. Note that each names the group to be reached and the idea to be communicated:

1.  We want to tell baby boomers that our store is **the** place to come for family cycling.

2.  Our plan is to let enthusiasts know that we have an extremely knowledgeable staff concerning mountain biking equipment and competition.

3.  We hope to increase our traffic among parents of toddlers to let them know we are the place to buy the first bike or trike.

4.  Our effort will be aimed at telling area teens where they can buy the hottest bicycle fashions.

5.  We are targeting area pediatricians to encourage them to send their clients to our store for helmets.

6.  We have a large customer base and our advertising will be aimed at increasing the number of times they visit per year.

7.  Currently, the store only draws from about a three-mile radius. We hope to use advertising to draw people from up to five miles away.

8.  We are changing our image from high-tech to family-friendly. We need to communicate with our new customers.

9.  Happily, we are very satisfied with our current sales and profits. We want to use advertising to maintain our present levels. We feel we can do this by reaching our existing customer base with reminder advertising.

After you have established who you hope to reach and what

you want to say, it becomes necessary to determine how much you will spend in time and money. Yes, time must be budgeted also, as retailing has the distinct advantage of being able to utilize both time and money to great advantage in promoting the business.

First, determine how much to spend. There are three well known methods for determining an advertising budget. The easiest is to use a percentage of sales from the year just past. The percentage is open to great debate. *Bicycle Dealer Showcase* generally runs an issue of its magazine each year that shows current average expenditures. The range might be from 2- 5%.

The second approach is to use a similar percentage of your projected sales. This school of thought would argue that you can't get your expected increase without paying the percentage on the increase also.

The final method is not quite so scientific. You work out several possible campaigns. You then price each of these out. Call them good, better, and best. The decision now becomes a business decision instead of a numbers game. There may be slightly more risk, but you can judge the results on your instincts about marketing rather than your management of the overall budget.

A variation of the third approach would begin with a launch of the "good" campaign, but be prepared to move to the "better" if sales and profits allow.

I personally am a great fan of using time as a substitute for money. In Chapter 6, "Twenty Five Ways to Sell More Tomorrow," many of the ideas show that bias. Except for Yellow Page advertising, I believe that the average retailer would get better results from hiring a part-time promoter than from any other expenditure, even if this employee was limited to a $1,000 a year for printing fliers and other small expenditures. This is not to say that hiring such a person is any easier than figuring out what will work in regular media. There must still be a commitment of supervision and constant evaluation of results.

Be certain to measure the results of all your advertising and promotion. Start by deciding what needs to occur for the campaign to be successful. Next, decide how you will measure the response. You might ask those who call or visit how they heard about you. You can include a coupon in your advertisement. Or you can merely chart the level of activity for the period of the campaign compared to a normal, but similar period.

## Advertising - Getting the Most Bang for Your Buck

Yellow Pages advertising used to be so simple. Less than ten years ago there was only one book, no second colors, no coupons, and no haggling over the rate. Only one thing remains the same ten years later. Yellow Page advertising is still the number one way to get new customers into your store.

Therefore, if your long-term or short-term goal is to increase new customer traffic, become more aggressive in your Yellow Page advertising. Research in depth the capability of competing books in your area. Ask other business associates for their opinion of the effectiveness of the coupons or the second ink color.

Don't hesitate to pick the brain of the representatives of the various phone book companies. Many of these salespeople have extensive backgrounds in such sales and can be a real help. However, they are on commission, and you should be wary of accepting all their claims without substantive back-up.

My general opinion is that you would do best to take a substantial ad in the "best" book, and a smaller ad in the other book or books, rather than an equal part in each. It is not clear to me that anything above a quarter page is substantially better than a quarter. However, you should make every effort to afford a quarter-page ad in the "best" book.

Unless you consider yourself an expert at advertising, hire an advertising professional for this ad. Remember you can usually only communicate one idea in an ad. This is also true for phone books. Many bicycle shop ads I've seen either become cluttered with too much information, or fail to give any reason to shop at that store.

Consider your own use of the Yellow Pages. How do you

decide which company to call or visit? Size of ad? Color? Probably your decision will have more to do with such issues as:

1. Do you believe they will have what I want?

2. Are they close by or easy to get to?

3. Can you get there during their hours of operation?

4. Are they friendly? Professional? (What is the image?)

Add your own thoughts to this list. This should help you know what you want in the ad. You will need a professional to tell you how to lay the advertisement out in such a way as the reader will see and understand the message.

Get an 800 number to advertise in your Yellow Page spread. These numbers are not that expensive today. If you can, get one that spells something. Ours is 800 BIKE REP. I never have to look up 800 FLOWERS. I promise you it will pay for itself many times over. People today like to be able to call businesses for free.

Ask your major bike line suppliers to co-op an ad which lists all area shops carrying that brand. If you carry two or more lines, try to get each to do so. The more times you are listed, the more likely you are to get called. If the supplier won't help out, consider joining forces with other shops who carry the line. One retailer I know in another industry shared expenses with two other shops and took a quarter page ad in all area phone books. She never could have afforded this exposure without the other shops' cooperation.

Use an answering machine or service for after hours. Indicate in the ad that your customers can leave a message twenty-four hours a day. People often decide they want something on Saturday evening at 9:00, and head for the phone book to see if anyone is open. If not, they have forgotten all about it by Monday. However, if someone called them back on Monday . . . .

The second most popular retail advertising today is taking place in the bicycle industry tabloids. Regional bicycle publications have sprung up all over the U.S. and they seem to be reaching their audience. If you have one or more of these tabloids in your marketing area, have their sales representatives come by with rates and readership data on their audience.

Industry tabloid advertising can become very tricky. Placement is very important, and is not necessarily meted out with total fairness. As with most phone books, the rates are very negotiable. New publications will sometimes give free advertising to prove their pull.

If your budget for all print advertising will be over $20,000 per year, you may want to see if a local advertising agency is willing to provide services. If you will spend less than that, you may be able to find a free lancer who will work by the hour.

As stated elsewhere (Chapter 6), beyond the Yellow Pages and tabloids, my preferences lean towards door hangers, mailings, and specialty advertising (water bottles, hats, stickers). However, I know of bicycle people who have had excellent results from bus bench ads, newspaper, radio, and even television.

Cable television can be remarkably inexpensive, but one dealer who has had a fairly aggressive campaign going for about a year feels that he has not quite broken even yet. He is willing to lose a little to build future business and establish the shop as the most aggressive in the area.

Because these media or so much more expensive, make certain that you know what you want to accomplish, quantify what "success" is, and measure results.

## Promotions That Work

Many promotions can be done for little or no money. Sometimes, they require a very small time commitment as well. I personally believe that these promotional ideas should form the basis of your marketing program. You probably can't do all of them, and certainly can't do all of them at once. However, I greatly encourage you to do as many as you can as often as you can, and add plenty more of your own.

1.  Sponsor regularly scheduled rides that start and end at your store. It is possible to do this with your involvement limited to organization. Set up times and routes. Promote these with

listings on your bulletin board, in the front window, and hand out a list to every new bicycle purchaser. In fact, ask any customer if they'd be interested in joining a ride, and give them a sheet, too. If you had ten rides of twenty people leaving your store each week, you wouldn't need any other advertising or promotion.

The gains from this type of activity are huge. First, people buy bikes to go riding. Once they buy a bike they don't know where to go, and they can never find anyone to go with them. If you provide both, you will keep people riding. If they ride, they invite more friends to participate in the sport, buy more accessories and clothes, and wear out equipment.

Second, it becomes easy for everybody to shop at your store if they are coming by once a week or so. They also become friends of the shop, which means that they will recommend others come by.

Third, if large groups are seen pedaling around town, other folks begin to figure it must be the thing to do, or are reminded that they have wanted to do it all along. Encourage your groups to wear matching shirts or some other insignia to help build their "club."

Fourth, people are looking for places (other than bars and through computers and personals) to meet other people. You could become the healthy meeting place for singles in your area.

To create even more interest in these rides, create different themes or groupings. You could have teens, young singles, career singles, families, hot shots, offroaders, mature adults, a lunch bunch, sunrisers, twenty milers, seniors and others.

Promote these specialty rides at places where these folks hang out: Teens through the high school newspaper, mature adults through the local community center or retirement homes, singles through ads at laundromats or in the personal want ad section. Promote all groups through free listings in the local paper and radio stations.

You may want one of your staff to ride with the group the first time out. However, unless you feel it is important to continue to involve staff in these rides (and I can think of plenty of good reasons to do so), establish a leader for each group, and help them get organized.

If you aren't already doing this, start tomorrow!

2.  Sponsor a major annual event. The list of possibilities is almost endless and so are the potential benefits. For instance you could organize a century, a sanctioned race for any of the various racing circuits, a benefit bike-a-thon (either in conjunction with the Jerry Lewis telethon or separately for some other cause), a triathlon or biathlon, a hill-climb competition on the steepest road in town, or any of a hundred other ideas that might be unique to your neighborhood.

These events take substantial amounts of planning, and can take two years or more to build momentum. However, if it's fun and well organized, you can easily end up with thousands of participants.

First, put together a plan. What will the event be? When will it be held? How many people will turn out? Where will it take place? Will there be a need for permits, licenses, insurance, police assistance, and the like? How many volunteers will be needed for planning and for the day of the event? What will these people be needed to do? What will be the budget? How will the event be advertised and promoted?

The next question is the most important . . . Who are the potential sponsors and providers of money and people? There is an almost endless list of possibilities, but you need to zero in on your direction.

For instance, it is quite possible to line up all the needed money and manpower for any event from your community. Start with the largest and best-organized community organization. In many cities this will be the local chamber of commerce. In others it might be the Rotary, Lions, Optimists, or other service club.

A second community source would be a major local corporation. Is there a company in town that is particularly friendly to the bicycle community, or that is always a leader in sponsoring local events? Those who already are involved in thes types of sponsorships are always the most likely to do another one.

Local charitable organizations are another great potential source of help. Unlike the others, their motive will be profit, but they will be a great source of manpower.

You may prefer to keep it in the family, and not ask your community for help. Instead, you might band together with other shops in your area, and seek financial assistance from bicycle industry sources and well known national sponsors of bicycling events.

Once you have targeted your preferred source of assistance, ask them for an opportunity to make a presentation of the idea at one of their membership meetings. It will help your prospects if you are able to line up support from one or more influential members or staffers before the meeting, but the important thing is to impress the membership with a great presentation.

As with all selling, you want to talk benefits. What is the event going to do for the community and for the organization you are pitching? The typical charitable organization or service club is looking to add membership, raise money for local concerns, and raise its profile in the community. Stress how this event can help to accomplish these ends.

National sponsors are hoping to sell more product, both short and long term. They also may be interested in the image that comes with being associated with bicycling. Finally, they are looking for national public relations opportunities. Will your event be so unique that the national press would have interest? Sell these types of ideas to the for profit sponsors.

Paying for the event is usually easier than amassing the necessary volunteers. Seed money can generally be provided by the various sponsors, in addition to your own store. Generally, it won't require much more than $1,000 to handle all the expenses prior to the actual event and the items that will be part of the event.

Sources of revenue to pay for advertising, brochures, street banners, police assistance, insurance, and all the other expenses directly related to the event can come from: tickets, advertising in the program, advertisements on the grounds of the events, sponsorships of individual participants in bike-a-thon-type event, sales of souvenirs such as water bottles, hats, and programs, sales of food, drinks, or other concessions, and sales of booth space in a mini-show to local and national companies wishing to sell or promote their products or services.

One of the most successful methods of raising charitable funds at a major event is through a raffle. It is reasonably easy to get local businessmen to donate small items to a charity raffle. The key to a successful one, however, is to get at least one business to give you a big item. Cars are best, but large-screen TV's, spas, and other high ticket items work well. Bicycles, of course, can be a very good top prize and are almost always among the second or third prizes.

In all of this, make certain that you are THE PRIMARY SPONSOR, or that you share the spotlight with only one other primary organization. All press releases should go out with a mention of your store, and preferably with a quote from you or one of your employees.

3.  Start a club, or take a club under your wing. Is there already an active Wheelman's club in your area? If not, start one. If yes, do they need a better place to meet? Is there room in your town for two such clubs? If not Wheelman, maybe a club for teenagers.

    This approach is different from the "ride" suggestion in Number 1 above. A club is brought together for more than participation in the sport. Many such clubs are the source of personnel for events, provide community assistance in other ways, or act as lobbyists for local bicycle causes such as bicycle lanes or mountain access.

4.  There are various types of promotions that can also double as a way to counterattack retailers who discount heavily. I hear from my bike shop owner friends that consumers are still asking for a discount. Moreover, I understand that some shops still discount the price of a bicycle. In fact, some retailers are discounting so deeply that other stores are reluctant to go that low.

Here are some approaches and solutions to the discounting situation:

Take away the competition's momentum. In other words, they started discounting, you followed; they went lower, you followed. You need to be the one who is controling the situation.

You can do this most effectively by **eliminating the consumer's ability to make direct comparisons.** If you and your competition are selling identical bicycles, what do you expect the consumer to do? Give you more money because you have a kind face?

If you have read Chapter 4, you should be able to get more money for a bicycle just by virtue of your superior selling skill. However, let's assume that the competition has read Chapter 4, also. Now what?

**Free service contract** - When you purchase a new TV at the department store, they offer you a 90-day warranty for free and a three year service contract for lots of money. Most consumers buy the service contract. When the service contract expires, someone from the store calls to see whether you'd like to renew the contract.

I believe that bike shops would do very well to begin offering a similar product. I've read in *Bicycle Business Journal* that a few shops have begun to do so. One was charging $39.95 for three years. (I surely hope this was limited to lubes and adjustments.) I think his amount was right, but it should have been for one year. $99.95 seems about right for three years. Remember, some folks will never be back. They'll move, sell the bike, or hang it up on the wall. Others will never need a repair beyond lubrication and tightening. Some very minor services can be given free, just to get the consumer to visit the shop once in a while (see below).

Once you have established this service, it now becomes a bargaining chip. Instead of dropping your price to $39.95, give away one year of service worth $39.95. Need a deeper discount to make the deal? Give two years.

**Create your own unique bicycle** - Equip a standard bike with Mr. Tuffy. Put up a sign that declares this to be a flat-proof bicycle.

You could even state that you will repair any flat for up to three years. Add twenty-five dollars to your regular price. The consumer can no longer make a comparison. You have a benefit that the other bike lacks.

You can create other unique bicycles by adding other features or upgrading parts. In many European countries, the lights, pump, and book rack are standard equipment on all bikes. What should be standard equipment in your store?

**Make your customer a member of your special club** - Take a page out of the success enjoyed by the membership discount clubs and now being followed by the bookstores. Start a customer club that provides discounts on products and services and other member benefits.

As with the service contract above, establish a value for this membership. The range is probably $10 to $29.95. Have a card printed up with your store name, the name of the club, and a place for the consumer's name on the front. On the back, list the benefits of membership.

You now have a new source of revenue, because you can actually sell these memberships. A great time to sell them is at the checkout. If the customer's purchases as a member would have been $7 less, offer to include today's transaction in the deal. If your membership is $10, the customer pays an extra $3 today for all the benefits.

You also have a way to give something away or add value to the bicycle. Give away the membership as part of every bike sale.

**Lifetime limited-service guarantee** - If you aren't already providing the customer with a free 90-day inspection, lube, and tightening, you should begin at once. I would even take this process out of the hands of the service department. Even the least mechanically oriented sales person can perform these duties.

When a bicycle comes in for a free inspection, have the next-available sales clerk perform these services on the spot. This creates an incredible customer service demonstration, and it provides the salesperson with a golden opportunity to sell.

While working on the bike, the salesperson should ask about the customer's experiences thus far with the bicycle. Where have they ridden? Have they experienced any problems with the bike? Are they interested in participating in store rides or joining a club? The information thus gathered can be used to provide more "need filling." For example, "Gosh John, for that type of riding, have you considered getting a light set? It's really dangerous to ride in the dark without proper lighting."

Now then, why wouldn't you want this service to be free, or almost free for the life of the bicycle? Possibly you would limit the customer to one free service per year. The dental plan I belong to provides one free cleaning per year. It keeps me coming to that dentist at least once every twelve months. No other dentist is going to see the cavity or suggest the need for crowns.

This could be one of the benefits of membership in your "Club." Or it could be a separate deal altogether. A third possibility would be to offer the service at a deep discount for bicycles purchased from you. If you normally charge $29.95 for a Spring tune-up, give anyone who has your sticker on their bike a 50% discount.

One last benefit of using the "Club" method or the free annual inspection is the opportunity to contact the customer on a regular basis through the mail or on the phone. "Hi, Andy. This is Bob over at Spoke Power. It's been a year since you've had your free, annual bike tune-up. If you'd like to bring it in, let's agree on a time so I can get you in and out real quick. Do you have a day this week that would be convenient?"

Hold a major sale - Many dealers have learned about the benefits of a spectacular weekend sales event. I have seen dealers amass sales equal to their best month in just three days. The concern that some felt about stealing future sales turned out to be not only unfounded, but the opposite of reality. Follow-up sales of clothing, accessories, and parts from new customers actually resulted in increased revenues following the event.

As of this writing there are three major national sales involving hundreds of shops. The oldest of these is the Super Sale organized by Catalyst Communications. Currently, approximately 200 dealers participate in the Spring and late Summer Super Sales. According to a company spokesman, there are openings in some parts of the country for additional dealers.

More recently, Schwinn and Trek have created "Cycle Madness" and "Trek Fest," respectively. These two sales are limited to dealers who sell the appropriate line of bicycles. This points to one major difference between Super Sale and the manufacturer-sponsored events. Super Sale does not promote any line of bicycles, while the other two do.

All three events have met with substantial success, and I recommend that all dealers check into the possibility of participating in these sales.

There are also promoters who put on individual sales. They are experts at designing advertisements, arranging media placements, consulting with you about what to sell and how much to discount. Most will also assist you in arranging discounts from suppliers.

If you should choose to attempt your own major sales event, here are a few ideas to keep in mind:

A.   Offer for sale those items that consumers already want. This will increase traffic, greatly increase the total revenue, create the impression of your store that you want consumers to have, and leave you with easy inventory to sell if you don't meet your projections.

Contrast this with trying to make sale items out of products you or your distributors are trying to unload. The consumer is far less likely to make a special trip, he is less likely to spend as much if he does come, he will perceive your store as selling unappealing products, and you may be a long time unloading excess inventory.

B.   Push brand names. You may even be better off to promote a product which you find less appealing, but which has a wanted brand, than to give a super big discount on an item you really like, but which the public doesn't know about. Save your pioneering efforts for normal business days. Major sales events are designed to move mountains of product and introduce your store to new customers.

C.  Don't buy products that you wouldn't otherwise carry. You will be calling your suppliers to ask for added discounts that you can pass along during your sale. You will want to buy the hottest items he carries. He will want to sell you something he has bunches of. If he is willing to take back what you don't sell, you may want to give it a shot. Otherwise, pass.

D.  Most of your discounts should be in the 25-40% range. Consumers find 10% to be uninteresting and a discount of 50% will raise a question about the quality of the merchandise. If you have made a great buy on something, and feel that 50% off would be a real barn-burner, make sure you explain your reason for this deep discount.

E.  Be sure to offer something for free. Water bottles with your name on them would be one good idea. Indeed, anything that has your name on it beats something that doesn't.

F.  Expect to spend as much as 20% of your expected revenue for advertising the sale. In other words, if you think you can generate $50,000 in sales, you should probably plan to spend $10,000 in advertising.

G.  Even if your first sale is less than what you hoped, continue to offer the sale annually if you can possibly afford it. These types of promotions tend to build over time. You should not be disappointed if your effort results in a revenue neutral weekend (no profit, no loss). While everyone would hope for and prefer a profit, this type of sale should be seen first as a business-builder with long lasting benefits.

H.  Be certain to produce a mailing list of the participants. It is very likely that those who visit will never have been in your store before. You will lose valuable potential if you do not follow up with some type of mailing to encourage them to return.

I.  Maintain a policy (with exceptions, of course) of having the customer return to your store during the following week to pick up any bikes purchased. First, it will be almost impossible for you to "make ready" those bikes that sell. Second, it is even less likely that you will have the time to instruct the buyer in proper use. Third, you want them to come back and buy the things they didn't buy at the sale.

**Become a teacher** - Offer to teach classes in various aspects of cycling at your local grade school, junior high, high school, junior college, college, YMCA, community recreation center, retirement center, or any other place where there might be twenty or thirty or more people who would like to learn more about cycling.

**Stage a publicity stunt** - The next section of this chapter tells all the details you'll ever need to know about how to get your store name in the paper. As an introduction I will now offer you a list of wild and crazy stunts you might be able to use to create big crowds and/or major media coverage. I once headed an organization that protested the installation of Diamond Lanes on the Santa Monica Freeway in Southern California. One of our stunts resulted in two-inch high headlines in every major Los Angeles newspaper and the number one spot on every TV news program. Why not you?

1.  Get the city to agree to block a centrally-located but relatively unimportant street. It should be at least 1,000 yards long. Hold a day-long series of "slow races." You know, the last one over the finish line wins. Break the competition into ages, sexes, or types of bikes. However, the day should conclude with an overall winner. By having the event last all day, it provides those who just happen to see the goings on to go get their bikes and give it a try. You will get press. The local paper here gives almost a full page of pictures and editorial to the annual bed race!

2.  Try to set a Guinness record at something. Longest wheely? Longest time on bike? Longest time on a unicycle? Fastest time for various distances? Most riders in drafting line? Most riders on one bike? Tallest rideable bicycle? Biggest rideable gear? Lightest bike? Remember, you want two results. First, a crowd to watch the attempt. Second, a full press publicity campaign.

3.  Bring a celebrity to town. Do you know somebody who knows

somebody who is a celebrity? Maybe you catch wind that a notable is passing through town on another errand. Who lives fairly close by, but not so close that they wouldn't be interesting? Does your geographic location offer an appeal to entice a star to come visit?

4.  Have a "pay what you think it's worth" sale. Limit this sale to two hours on a Saturday afternoon. You may also want to limit the sale to accessories and clothing. Make sure that everything in the store has a price sticker reflecting its normal retail value. You'll be surprised at how many people will pay close to sticker and how few will really rip you off. Keep in mind that even if your losses reached $1,000 for those two hours, the publicity will be worth it.

5.  Organize a "bicycle-only" day. Work with the city council and the chamber of commerce to take a role in the national smoke-out and have a day when everyone is encouraged to leave cars at home. Call on other anti-auto organizations such as the Sierra Club to back you up. Involve other bike sellers in your area, but make sure you get all the publicity. Point out to the city fathers that this will likely bring nationwide publicity to your town. Promote the idea as being valuable for the statement it will make, but it should also be seen as having a component of fun to it.

6.  How about a two-for-one publicity stunt? First, offer to pay $10 cash for any used bicycle regardless of condition, type, style, or age. Indicate that you want to help the community clean up its garages and backyards of rusting bicycle hulks. The news release should be full of fun. Establish a period (one day, a week, a month) during which the offer is good.

As the owners bring their bikes in, offer them $20 towards a new bike if they prefer. However, be very ready to make good on your $10 cash offer.

After you have collected all these used bicycles, donate the entire lot to neighborhood poor children. Check each of them to ensure their safety. You may want to involve a local charitable organization or service club in making these kinds of repairs or even spiffing them up a bit. If you do, sell this organization the needed parts at cost.

Hopefully, you will end up with a hundred used bikes or more. Have the newspapers run public service announcements and/or a feature articles about your intent to give them all away. The photo opportunities are endless. Pick a day for the distribution, and invite the press again.

## Public Relations is Almost Free

It isn't necessary to stage anything quite so elaborate as the above to get some ink in your local paper, or even a little TV coverage. You can do quite well by letting the press know about many of the things you might consider mundane.

AC International recently got five inches in the *Los Angeles Times* telling about Mr. Tuffy. The article listed six local bike shops that carry the product. The column is syndicated and will run in many papers nationwide.

**This story had absolutely no news value.** Editorial writers for newspapers need copy. They have to create huge amounts of material every day. Your job is to help them all you can. To get your ideas flowing, let me list a few subjects that are likely to get published:

1. New products, or products about which the public isn't well-informed.
2. Any type of event as listed above.
3. Send in your schedule of free rides every week.
4. If your club is having a speaker, send in a release.
5. Did you or one of your employees win something? Write it up.
6. Write a story on the owner. How he or she got into the business.
7. Are police in your area using bikes? Work with them on an article.
8. General trends in bicycling are always of interest.

9. Tips on repairs, preventing flats, or proper locking always get press.

Create a list of media in your area. This should include daily, weekly, and advertiser-type newspapers. The smaller the paper, the more likely it will be to run anything you send. Local radio and TV stations should be on the list. Newspapers put out by schools, colleges, or large employers are generally very well-read. If you are in an area served by one of the bicycle industry tabloids, it would be an obvious user of your material.

Other industries have similar tabloids. Check your phone book under "newspapers" for possible listings. Write articles for these which would tie bicycles to their subject matter.

## How to Prepare a Release

You do not have to be a Hemmingway to create a press release. In fact, news reporting requires a no-nonsense writing style that is fairly easy to imitate. There are a few basic rules to preparing your news release that will follow the custom of the industry and increase your chances of getting ink.

1. Have the release typewritten or computer generated on 8 1/2" X 11" white paper stock. It should be double-spaced.

2. The top of the page should indicate the urgency of the news. If the information must be printed immediately to be of value, use large bold letters across the top of the page to say "**FOR IMMEDIATE RELEASE.**" Don't use this line unless you only want the material considered for that day's news. If the paper doesn't have the space that day, it may get tossed.

   Otherwise use the terms **"PRESS RELEASE"** or **"DATED MATERIAL"** depending upon whether the information could be run anytime or should be run close to the date of an event.

3. Try to provide a local paper at least five days to print dated material.

4. In the heading or at the very top of the material, indicate the name of a contact person that can be reached for further

information or clarification. Include a phone number where that person can be reached. Be certain to include the name and address of your store.

5.  Headline writing is an art. If you think you can pull off a clever one, take your best shot. You may be better off to keep it simple and clear.

6.  The first paragraph should include the famous five W's: Who, what, where, when, and why. Some add an H, how. While this is a time-honored method of writing press releases, I would encourage you to find something catchy to say in the first sentence. If it can be catchy and still include some or all the five W's, better yet.

7.  The second and subsequent paragraphs fill in the details about the first. The more complete the information, the better the editor will like it. This means less work for him.

8.  Quote yourself. According to Jim Bond, owner of Double O Seven Cyclery, "The best way to stop flats is using tire liners, such as Mr. Tuffy."

9.  If there are two pages, be certain to write "more" at the bottom of the first page, not "1." You should then write "page 2 of 2" at the bottom of the second page. Most press releases should be less than one page. Only a feature article should be more than two pages. At the end of the release, write "-30-."

10. It is a very good idea to send a short cover letter on company letterhead. This shows that you are a current or potential advertiser. In addition, you make the material offered more personal. Call ahead to find out who releases should be sent to. There may be different editors for different types of material. The city editor usually gets immediate releases. A lifestyle editor may get releases on new products.

11. Follow up to make certain that your release was received. Don't be pushy about whether it will be used. Ask whether there were any questions not answered by the material. With any luck, the

editor will let you know whether and when the article will appear. If the editor acts as if he will use the information, but hasn't given you a date, you may ask when he thinks it will run.

12. Don't get discouraged. Some material will be used and some won't. You will likely find yourself amused by how some really good stuff gets passed over and other releases you thought were not big deals get printed. It may only have to do with which day the information was received, and how much space the editor needed to fill.

One last thought on publicity. Editorial material is ten times more likely to be read and believed than advertising. Therefore, if you spend $100 worth of time to get a release in the paper that uses the space of a $100 dollar ad, you will get $1000 dollars worth of benefit.

"It Says Now You Have To Have A Note From
Your Doctor And Your Mother!"

# CHAPTER 8

# PERSONNEL MANAGEMENT ISN'T FOR COWARDS

I'd love to ask bicycle dealers for a list of their least favorite tasks in running a retail establishment. If you'd like to cast your ballot, send it along to my publisher, Info Net Publishing. When we get enough of a response, I'll write an article about it for one of the trade magazines.

My guess is that a very close second behind washing the commode would be hiring a new employee. This is not to say that most entrepreneurs aren't excited and proud about the fact that they can help folks make a living. It is to say that hiring, training, motivating, disciplining, compensating, and firing employees can be a real trial at times.

The title for this chapter is borrowed from a book by Dr. James Dobson, a best selling author of child rearing books. His title was only slightly different, substituting "Parenting" for "Personnel Management." In many regards the two are not so different. In reviewing the list of management tasks related to employees offered at the end of the previous paragraph, you could say about children: birthing, training, motivating, disciplining, paying for, and getting shed of can be a real trial at times.

## The Coming Labor Shortage

Let me start this section by dramatically increasing your anxiety about this task. The USA and many other Western industrial nations are on the verge of the most serious labor shortage since

World War II. This is not a prediction. It is a fact. Recent history and basic demographic (population) studies will provide you with all the proof any skeptic could need:

1. Starting in 1964, there was a drop in births of almost 1,000,000 babies per year. This trend was not reversed until 1982. Therefore, as of 1994, there will be 10,000,000 fewer entry-level employees (ages 20-30) than there were in 1984. This trend will continue until 2002 when the first members of the echo baby boom reach age 20. At that point there will be 18,000,000 fewer adults between the ages of 20 and 38 than there were in 1984.

2. You shouldn't need any more proof than that. However, some of you are thinking we will make that up with increased immigration. Without even turning to statistics, I can't imagine that any reader would think that our country would be able to manage additional migration of that magnitude.

   Most nations of the world who have used immigration as a method to increase the size of their work force have later come to regret it. The USA will rightly continue to offer itself as a refuge for those seeking a better way of life, but an increase in immigration will not cure the coming labor shortage.

3. Women added huge numbers of extra workers to the labor pool between the middle sixties and the late eighties. That trend has now reversed, with women returning home in very large numbers. It is unlikely that women will ever represent a larger percentage of the available pool of workers than they do today.

4. For more proof, let's take a short walk down memory lane. In the recession of 1981, we had double digit unemployment. In the recession of 1991, we never reached 8%. That good news was as a result of shrinkage in the number of new laborers available.

5. Just before the recession of 1991, we had the first taste of a labor shortage with McDonald's, other fast food chains, hotels, movie theaters, and other businesses needing low paid workers in a real panic. Their solutions included:

A.  More automation

B.  Hiring retirees

C.  Paying more salary (sometimes a lot more)

D.  Stepped-up recruiting

E.  New benefit schemes

The only thing that kept the "taste" of labor shortage from becoming a full blown crisis was the recession of 1991. By 1994 or 1995, we will be back to the aggravation of 1989. By 1996-7, it will be THE news topic, replacing crime, drugs, and the deficit.

It is critical that you begin plotting a strategy now to deal with the potentially crippling effects of the competition for unskilled workers and middle managers. The very core employees of most bike shops will be the least available and the most in demand.

The key element in that strategy for most bicycle retailers will be changing their approach on personnel issues from seat-of-the-pants to professional management. In other words, from hanging a "help wanted" sign on the door and hiring the first soul who walks in that appears to have all his or her faculties to a continuous plan for recruitment, interviewing, training, motivating, disciplining, and compensating employees.

## Hiring as a Part of Managing Personnel

Andrew Carnegie, who founded and built Carnegie Steel into what would eventually become US Steel, is often sighted as maintaining that if you took away his buildings and his machinery, but left him with his people, he would be able to rebuild the enterprise in short order. It would appear that most (though by no means all) bike shops would feel almost the opposite. As long as they have their lease and their lines, almost any employee will do.

If the individual who has charge of personnel decisions in a bike shop were to spend four hours per week in the careful hiring and training of its people, the results would be immediate, obvious, and impressive.

For the purposes of this chapter, let's use the sales clerk as an example. We could use the mechanic, bookkeeper, manager or other common bike shop employee, but I think it will be hardest to find qualified sales clerks that will be long-term employees.

The beginning of any hiring practice is the determination of the qualifications for the position and the job description. As in any relationship between two people, the more that each knows about what to expect and what is expected, the better chance of success.

In a sales clerk, you might list qualifications such as outgoing, relaxed in dealing with people, ENTHUSIASTIC, energetic, goal oriented, well- groomed, respectful, high self-esteem, intelligent, and with sales experience. Your list could be longer, although be careful not to include any qualifications which could be seen as discriminatory.

It will not be easy to find a candidate that will get top marks in every category. It will be even more difficult to convince one who does get good marks to work for the low wages often offered by the bicycle industry. Leaving wages aside for a moment, however, if we don't have some idea of the things we want, we can't even come close.

A job description may seem like an odd idea to the smallest shops. Where the person to be hired will be the second of two, counting the owner, it may seem as if a single line would do: "Whatever is needed that I don't want to do." However, whether this employee will be your first or your fortieth, it is critical to lay out an understanding of what will be asked of them, and what is expected. Here is a sample job description.

## Job Description for Sales Clerk at Bobby's Bike Barn

1. Arrive one hour before opening each day to make certain that showroom is completely ready for customers. This includes: restocking shelves; cleaning and dusting bikes, showcases, and window display; sweeping front walk; general policing of all other areas, being certain that all bikes are tagged; and preparing cash register.

2. Checking for out-of-stocks in important categories to serve as

back-up to automatic purchasing system.

3. Approaching all customers within one to two minutes of arrival, if not already working with a customer.

4. Providing courteous and knowledgeable sales help to customers. Your goal should be to close 90% of those customers who come to the shop intending to purchase a bicycle.

5. Use of slow periods to restock and police entire showroom, so as to maintain an excellent appearance of selling areas at all times.

6. Also use slow periods to learn more about product through reading of packaging, brochures, trade and consumer magazines, and industry retailing books. For maximum opportunity for advancement, it is recommended, though not required, that all sales clerks continue to educate themselves on their own time as well. This could include magazines, books, tapes, and seminars on specific industry topics such as selling and managing.

7. Hours are 9:00 a.m. to 6:00 p.m., Tuesday-Saturday, with an hour for lunch. This schedule is subject to change, and mandatory overtime is likely.

8. All employees are to be neat, clean, and well groomed always.

Once you have developed the job description and the qualifications, you are ready to round up some candidates. The following is intended as a comprehensive list of approaches to maximizing the pool of potential people from which to choose what can become a great asset for your company.

1. In my experience the best place to find good people is among my existing circle of employees, friends, business associates, and acquaintances. As soon as we decide to hire a new employee, we let everyone around us know what we are looking for. For example, we recently needed to hire a receptionist. Within one day we had two outstanding candidates who were friends of current employees.

This method is tempered to some degree by the potential problems of hiring people who you know, or friends and family of current employees. However, AC International now has over 50 employees, including family of the owners, husbands and wives, and numerous extended families, and we have less turnover and problems from these groups than we do from hiring strangers.

My own approach is to keep an "A" list of people in my acquaintance who I think would make excellent employees. Sometimes I'll even let them know that I hope to hire them someday. Most, if not all, are flattered by such a statement. As a position comes closer, I scan the "A" list to see if I already have someone in mind that could do it. If there is one or more, I begin preliminary conversations with the person to see where they stand.

If I don't have anybody on my list, I begin by asking my most trusted employees and friends for ideas. If those wells dry up, I move to lower echelon employees, suppliers and their salesmen, and other networking among the trade.

I believe that this type of personal hiring will be the most important method of staying ahead during the labor shortage. This is because it is proactive. Those who wait until an employee leaves or a need arises to begin the search will find themselves going without for long stretches.

2. Community placement programs. I am not a fan of the unemployment department, especially during a labor shortage. Generally, the lower the unemployment rate, the more likely it is that those who are still getting an unemployment check are doing so on purpose. You don't need those folks.

However, many states, counties, and cities have created referral programs for hard to place workers or those who have come through some type of rehabilitation program. Sometimes you will even be reimbursed a portion of their pay if they last for 90 or 180 days. While you need to use every bit as much judgment in hiring someone from this source as you do from any other, it can bring excellent results. Importantly, not many employers are aware of these programs, which increases your chances for finding excellent candidates.

3. High School and College placement programs. The most effective method is to get to know the folks who run these placement departments. They are often able to steer the best applicants to the businesses they like the best. They will also help as much as possible to screen what they perceive to be undesirable candidates.

Many college courses have mandatory internship programs. The student is required to gain real-life experience by working for a company in their field of study. They may be able to earn a small wage for this, or they may do it for no income. Commonly, today's enthusiastic intern becomes tomorrow's ideal employee.

4. Temporary services. AC International's number one source of new employees is temp services. There are two types of people who offer their skills through such services: those who truly want to work on a temporary basis, and those who are doing so only until they find permanent employment.

There are also two types of temporary services agencies. Some require that you sign a contract stipulating that if you hire one of their employees on a permanent basis, you will either pay the agency a lump sum, or continue to pay them for the employee's time for a minimum number of weeks. These arrangements are usually true for both white collar and skilled positions.

The other type of agency has no such requirements. They are usually primarily in the business of supplying unskilled labor.

In both instances, you will generally pay very little premium above what you would otherwise pay for the employee if on your own payroll. First, the agencies don't pay very well. Second, they are taking care of all the overhead items such as Social Security, Workers' Compensation, and other benefits.

The beauty of using temporary services agencies is fourfold.

First, you are able to take a look at the actual work habits of an employee without making any commitment. If you don't like the first person sent by the agency, send 'em back and ask for another. . . and another . . . and another.

Second, you can usually get someone with pretty good skill at a moment's notice. Therefore, the agency provides you with a back-up situation for unexpected employee leave-taking.

Third, it is by far the least expensive method from the standpoint of the hiring process itself. There is no cost and very little time to arrange for someone to be sent over. There is no need to interview five or ten people. There is no immediate problem of determining appropriate compensation. (And by the way, the agency's proposed compensation is negotiable.)

Fourth, you can use these agencies for seasonal workers with no specific intent to hire permanently. If, however, you have a standout among these seasonal workers, you may decide to make a permanent hire.

The only negatives are the possible extra training time and the possibility of losing a worker to another opportunity during the trial time. However, if you find that the agency is sending you poor recruits, switch agencies. Most towns have several companies in that business.

5. Advertise in industry publications. Almost every part of the US now has a tabloid newspaper for bicycle enthusiasts. If you feel that the position you are offering would be enhanced by having a bicyclist holding that job, rather than someone who doesn't know a grip shift from a bar-end mirror, this is the way to go. You should generally plan further in advance, since it may be 30 days or longer until your ad will appear. Some bike shops keep a perpetual ad in these newspapers and constantly compile names of potential workers.

You should also keep your other requirements firmly in mind. It has been our general experience that we are better off to have a highly-skilled salesman who needs to learn what the parts of a bicycle are, than to have a great rider who needs to learn how to sell.

The last step in the management of the hiring process is the interview and hiring decision. I don't believe that there are any interviewing concepts that are unique to the bicycle shop business, so I will leave that aspect to other forums. (*When Friday Isn't Payday* has an in-depth offering in this area.) However, I do believe that the interview should be the first step in the training process. This means that to maximize the potential of any new hire, there are certain other preparations that you should accomplish before the first interview.

When you are discussing someone's potential for winning a position with your firm, you will have their attention in a way rarely to be duplicated again. First, they may need or at least badly want this job. Otherwise, why would they be there? Second, they are interviewing you as well. Most people who sign on with a company hope it will be long term. Third, their ego is fully exposed. There are few things more hurtful than being turned down for a job.

Therefore, a soon as the interview reaches a point where you believe this candidate is clearly in the running, use that focused attention to explain your philosophy, your corporate mission, and certain goals. Of course, if you haven't followed the admonitions of previous chapters, you may not have a philosophy, a mission, or any goals.

By providing the future employee with this information at a time when his mind is going to make an almost perfect snapshot of your every word and movement, you will save yourself much future effort to ingrain these principles.

## Training and motivating employees.

Now that you've gone through the pregnancy and the birth (so to speak), you are approaching the critical time in the life of your newborn employee. The effect of what you do in the next ninety days is similar to the effects of what parents do in the first five years. Your infant employee is going to be absorbing data about you, your business, and his role in his new environment. This period will set the stage for all future behavior by the new hire.

It is more than a homily to suggest that people under your supervision will be far more influenced by what you do than what you say. By the end of ninety days, your trainee will have made certain observations and developed certain feelings:

1. I am liked, tolerated, or not liked.

2. I am important, not very important, or a mere cog.

3. This is exciting, not too bad, or just a paycheck.

4. The company has energy, is plain vanilla, or is going nowhere.

5. The owner is involved, somewhat concerned, or not interested.

6. I know what to do, I think I know what to do, I'm faking it.

7. My superior cares about my success or doesn't.

8. The company is interested in building a business, making money, other.

9. I can make a difference. I can't make a difference. I don't care.

How do your employees feel at the end of 90 days? How do they feel right now? Is it too late to turn them around?

Different kinds of employees with different needs respond best to different types of managers. Some folks are very autonomous and prefer less direct supervision. Some are very social and work best in an environment that is fun loving and friendly. Still others like clear cut rules and boundaries, and are most at home with a stern taskmaster. But all employees look for consistency and integrity.

Spend at least a couple of hours the first day with any employee who will report directly to you. Discuss the job description in detail until you are convinced that you are both in complete understanding of what is expected, and how it can be achieved. Introduce the new person to all other employees with enthusiasm for both the work of the existing crew and the hopes for the new addition.

Go over the specific details of immediate tasks to be performed.

Let the employee do half the talking. Encourage questions, observations, and suggestions. The more they get to talk, the better they will feel about you. If you knock down their ideas now, you'll make it harder for them to come forward later.

For the first few weeks, take at least a few minutes every day to sit down and go over questions, concerns, and ideas that have come up. Use this time to give first impressions of the work produced, the work habits observed, and the attitudes expressed in the early going.

Make extra certain in these early discussions that all criticism is constructive, and preferably sandwiched between praise. Don't be afraid to ask what the employee likes and doesn't like. These early observations can be very beneficial to an evaluation of your overall management style, and if learned early enough in the new relationship can be dealt with.

At AC International most new hires are brought in about 50¢ to $1.00 per hour below our target for that position. We explain that there is a ninety day probationary period, and that if we are both happy with one another at the end of that time, their salary will be increased.

This creates in the employee a major incentive to perform well during that probation. These early habits are pretty well ingrained by the end of 90 days.

The motivation of an employee after probation is worthy of an entire book. However, let's take a quick look at the most likely methods for a bike shop environment.

1.  Use a split-fee method of paying service workers. The employee may make somewhere between 25-33% of the ticket against minimum wage. This percentage could be based on years on the job, total volume of output, or many other methods. Generally, if the service employees were to be paid this way on repairs and upgrades, they would be paid piecework on set-ups.

2.  Pay commission against minimum wage for sales clerks. Alternatively, pay a bonus above minimum wage for reaching

certain goals. These goals can be set by management or by the employee with the approval of management.

3.  Establish a bonus pool based on profitability. Be certain that your accounting procedure is accurately measuring profitability before you try this one. If you are uncertain, but like the team concept, establish a bonus pool that pays off when the shop hits certain volume targets.

4.  Use spontaneous bonuses for excellent work. Handing an employee $20, $50, or even $100 out of the blue for a job well done will inspire that person for a week or more.

5.  Have an employee of the week, month, or year. While it is great to give a cash gift or other prize along with the recognition, you can get as good or better result from buying a perpetual plaque and adding names each month, while displaying a picture for that period of the winner.

You might also consider a special pin the employee wears with his name tag to identify him as the employee of the month. Customers also will enjoy knowing that they are being served by the best employee on the staff.

## Compensation Considerations

While ideas from this section are intertwined with the money motivation ideas in the previous section, the basic compensation issue will be one of the important issues of the coming labor shortage. If you are forced to pay too much for your labor, you could easily end up losing money in an otherwise great sales year.

People go to work and stay on the payroll of companies where they feel needed and appreciated. The amount of money in the check is important, but secondary.

**Profit in a labor-intensive business is a function of productivity, not pay scale.**

Put those two items together and what do you get? Your management of the facility is the real issue. It is possible to find people who will be thrilled to work for you in a supercharged atmosphere at less than the market pay. Or you could have folks who are paid well over the market who will leave first chance they get to go where they'll get some strokes.

It is also possible to pay one sales clerk $35,000 a year very profitably and another $10,000 to lose you money. It is not only possible, it is happening in bike shops at this very moment. That is why I am such an advocate of commissions or bonuses. At AC International, every person is part of a bonus plan that rates their performance every two weeks. Everyone - the receptionist, art director, purchasing agent, machine operators, bookkeepers, and office manager - they all make most or all the potential bonus on every check.

Most compensation experts will tell you that each hire should be evaluated in terms of the market rate for the position, the experience and capabilities of the employee, and the ability of the company to pay. There can be very little argument with this guideline. However, it could lull an owner into thinking he should follow the lead of most bike shops and hire anyone who is breathing that will take minimum wage.

Successful shops will hire the best person they can find for each position, pay them a negotiated wage that ensures their financial well-being, and incentivize their position, so that both the shop and the employee can benefit from extraordinary effort.

## A Complete Bicycle Shop Employee Manual

Very few shops have developed an employee manual. It is a tedious task at best, and given that there always seem to be far more important tedious tasks than this one confronting the average retailer, it never gets done.

However, an employee handbook can be a very beneficial tool for motivating and managing employees. It provides evidence of professionalism and concern. The handbook spells out issues that could otherwise create misunderstandings if not written down. Finally, the guidelines in the handbook can forestall legal problems if a company can show evidence of having communicated certain policies concerning discrimination and harassment.

With that in mind I have constructed a model Employee Manual designed to work for a bike shop. There will be things you may wish to change or leave out altogether. Your policy may be very different on issues such as vacation, sick leave and the like. However, for those of you who have wanted to offer such a manual, but were bogged down in the detail, you should be able to read through this one, make the appropriate changes, have it typed up, copied and distributed. For the few extra dollars it will cost you, I would highly recommend putting the contents into a three ring binder and having your company name stenciled on the front.

## EMPLOYEE HANDBOOK FOR HOLY SPOKES BIKE SHOP

## INTRODUCTION

We are very pleased that you have decided to join our organization. It is our hope that you will find the Holy Spokes Bike Shop to be an enjoyable place to earn a living. It is the policy of the management to maintain an open door at all times to provide you with an opportunity to discuss any aspect of your employment you wish.

This handbook has been developed to provide you with a guideline to our employment policies and the benefits extended to you. These policies and benefits are subject to change by the management at any time and do not represent a contract between employer and employee.

## COMPANY MISSION STATEMENT

The Holy Spokes Bicycle Shop is dedicated to the premise of improving the health and happiness of this community through sales of the finest bicycles and bicycle accessories. This image is further developed through the spotless appearance of our stores and employees. We are first and foremost interested in helping people, whether they are our customers or our employees.

As an employee of this firm, we expect you to help us work

toward our goals as stated in the mission statement. We welcome your ideas as to how we can best reach those goals.

We are an equal opportunity employer. It is our goal to ensure that no employee or applicant is ever discriminated against in any decision about hiring or promotion on the basis of sex, age, race, religion, color, marital status, disability (unless job related), or other legally determined status. If you believe that any such discrimination has occurred concerning your status or any other employee's or applicant's status, please bring it directly to the attention of the president.

## YOUR PAY

### Hourly Employees

A.  You must check in and out with your supervisor before and after your shift, and for your lunch break. Be certain they initial your time sheet.

B.  Your time will be determined in 15 minute increments. If you are more than five minutes late, it will be counted as 15 minutes.

C.  You will be paid time and one-half for <u>authorized</u> overtime up to four hours per day. Double time will be paid for authorized overtime above four hours per day, twenty hours per week, and for all  recognized holidays.

D.  You will be paid each Friday at the end of your shift. No paychecks will be handed out under any circumstances until the end of shift.

### Salaried Employees

A.  The workday is from 9:00 am to 6:00 pm with an hour for lunch. You may speak to your supervisor about possible variations of this schedule on a temporary or permanent basis.

B.  There is no payment for overtime. However, to the extent that a salaried employee must put in substantial extra hours, we will make available compensatory time off.

C. You will be paid twice each month. Payday will be on the first and sixteenth of the month.

## PERFORMANCE REVIEWS

Twice each year you will participate in a performance review. Your supervisor will provide you with an evaluation of your performance in the past six months and make recommendations for improvement. The supervisor will also ask for your input as to how the company can help you to improve in your position.

The review also provides an opportunity to consider your rate of pay. In general, the Spring review will be the time that deserving employees will receive increases based on performance.

The company has a policy of preferring to promote from within. The review will also provide you with an opportunity to let us know if there is another position within the company that you would like to work toward.

## BENEFITS

### Vacation

A. After you have been with the company for one year, you are entitled to one week of paid vacation. No vacation pay is earned until you have completed your first year. This vacation may be taken any time during the second year of employment with your supervisor's consent as to the specific dates.

B. During the second year you will begin to earn vacation time at the rate of 5/6ths of a day per month. You may use this time as you wish with your supervisor's consent as to specific dates.

C. After ten years, you will earn vacation time at the rate of 1 and 1/4 day per month.

D. You may not take vacation pay instead of the vacation time itself, except as part of any termination.

E. Part-time employees will not begin to earn vacation until they have worked a minimum of 1,000 hours per year. The amount of vacation earned will be determined on a percentage basis of hours worked compared to full-time or 2,000 hours per year. (e.g., an employee working 1,500 hours would earn 3/4th of the vacation of a full-time employee.)

---

## Holidays

---

### We observe the following holidays:

New Year's Day

Memorial Day

Fourth of July

Labor Day

Thanksgiving (2 days)

Christmas (1 and 1/2 days)

New Year's Eve (1/2 day)

A. Full-time employees are eligible to receive full pay for these days if they have worked the days before and after the holiday or have an excused absence for those days missed.

B. Part-time employees will receive pay for these holidays on the basis of the percentage of time worked on the other days in that pay period, or the percentage of hours worked year-to-date, whichever is higher.

C. The company will determine, at its discretion, which day any holiday will be observed if the holiday falls on a non work day.

## Sick Pay

After you have been with the company for 90 days, you are eligible for sick pay. This will be earned at the rate of one-half day per month. You may accumulate sick pay from year to year if not used. At the end of your fifth year, if you have accumulated at least 15 days of sick pay, you may exchange all or part of this accumulation for 50% of its value in pay. At the end of each year, thereafter, you may take 50% payment for any accumulated sick days.

1.  Approved sick days include: personal illness, the illness of a dependent child or parent where no other caregiver is available, the death of an immediate family member, visits to the doctor or dentist (two hours).

    Immediate family includes: Spouses, parents, brothers, sisters, children, grandparents, and in-laws in the same categories.

2.  Individuals who are found to have taken sick time which does not conform to the above are subject to dismissal.

## Health Plan

We are happy to provide all of our full time, permanent employees with full medical coverage. Details of the plan are available from the bookkeeper.

1.  You are eligible to participate in the plan after you have completed 90 days with the company.

2.  The company will pay 70% of the premium for coverage of the employee. The company will pay 50% of the premium for coverage of the employee's spouse and dependent children.

3.  **If you do not accept your option to join the plan at the end of your 90 day introductory period, you will not be able to join until the next general enrollment period.**

# WORK RULES

1. You are expected to be at work on time each day for which you are scheduled. If you are going to be late or absent, notify your supervisor at the earliest possible time. If you call and your supervisor is not available, leave a message indicating your intentions. Unexcused lateness or absence, or absence without notice, are cause for dismissal.

2. You are entitled to an unpaid meal break of either a half-hour or one hour depending on your schedule. You are also entitled to two ten minute breaks, one in each half of the day. You are expected to limit these breaks to the amount of time allowed. Failure to do so may result in disciplinary procedures and/or termination.

3. In the interest of the health of all employees and our customers, there will be no use of any tobacco products on the premises.

4. The company will not tolerate the use of alcohol, any illegal drug, or the abusive use of any legal drug while the employee is on the premises. The company will treat any such use as it does any other handicap or disability. The company reserves the right to terminate any employee whose use of any of the above results in danger to himself, his co-workers, or the public, or who is unable to perform his job requirements

5. The company believes that harassment of any type is counter-productive to the company's best interests. Therefore, any employee found to be harassing a fellow employee will receive a week without pay for the first offense and immediate termination for any further such offense.

   Harassment includes any activity by one person which would cause a reasonable person to feel uncomfortable to the point of emotional distress. A short list of possible activities that might cause such distress includes: statements, slurs, threats, or derogatory comments about another individual's race, ethnic background, color, religion, age, or sex; unwelcome sexual jokes, teasing, advances, or requests for sexual favors; any sexual touching; unwarranted slurs, threats, or derogatory comments regarding the work of an employee by his supervisor. Good disciplining does not include harassment.

Any employee who feels that they are a victim of such harassment should immediately report any such behavior directly to the president. However, if the employee would feel more comfortable discussing any such issue with a manager other than the president, they should feel free to do so. The manager must bring the matter to the attention of the president.

6. The company has a zero tolerance approach with regard to employee stealing in any form.

   A. Any employee caught stealing **ANY** property belonging to the company, other employees, guests, or vendors of the company **WILL BE IMMEDIATELY TERMINATED.** When appropriate the company will also prosecute such matters to the fullest extent of the law.

   B. Personal telephone calls outside our local dialing area, and/or on company time are both forms of stealing. Employees found to be making such calls without permission will be disciplined or terminated.

   C. Abuse of expense accounts will be considered the same as theft.

7. The company has established rules regarding the safe operation of materials and equipment. Employees found to be violating such rules will be subject to disciplinary action and/or termination depending on the seriousness of the violation.

8. Flagrant misconduct, violation of company policies, or insubordination are also conducts which may result in disciplinary action or termination.

   Discipline for the above may include, but is not limited to: verbal warning, written warning, time off without pay, or termination.

## CHAPTER 9

# THE POWER OF PURCHASING

More profit is made by buying right than by selling right. This sage advice has been passed down from generation to generation among merchants. However, many first-time owners opening businesses during the past decade have not had the development of good buying skills as part of their training. To understand the full meaning of this concept, let's take a look at a few examples.

For most bicycle dealers, the bicycle itself is still the number one source of gross sales income and therefore the single largest category of purchasing. How do the purchase decisions you make on bicycles affect the ultimate performance of your business?

## IN STYLE

First, your store will be judged by your customers and your current and future suppliers by the merchandise it keeps, especially the bike lines. Other than the look of your storefront and interior, no other aspect of your business will create more of an immediate impression. Only the personality and attitude of your staff will have a more long-lasting effect.

Therefore, the selection of bike lines has a major effect on your long-term success. To the extent that you purchase bicycle brands that are "in step" with the customer base you're seeking to attract, you'll benefit with a positive image. However, if you are perceived to be selling product which is out of touch or out of style, you can lose customer base very rapidly.

Be very careful in your evaluation of where you stand on this issue. If you and your staff are excellent at selling, and offer quality service, you may be able to maintain good closing percentages for a long time . . . even with the wrong product line. (You've heard the line about selling refrigerators to Eskimos.) Spend time and energy researching and listening to your customers regarding trends.

Your reputation for carrying the "right" bicycle line has long-term repercussions. The short-term results of purchasing the wrong line can be devastating long before your image is affected. Carrying "dead" inventory isn't part of the fast track to profitability. While no crystal ball is perfect, the more energy you put into predicting the direction bicycles are heading, the more likely you are to avoid a large purchasing error.

What do you do if you should get "stuck" with "dead" product? Here is more sage advice from generations of merchants: "The earliest loss is the best loss." Get rid of your "dogs" as quickly as possible. Here are several reasons why:

1.  They will never be worth more than they are now. Rather, they will continue to decline in value as time goes on. Don't be timid about your price reduction. Price these units to sell . . . and sell NOW!

2.  The longer they sit on your floor, the more they cost you. Once you have sold them, the dollars you collect can be used to purchase "the right stuff."

3.  They look bad on your floor. The faster you move them out, the less likely they are to sully your reputation. You and your staff may also have your attitude affected by being faced with "the mistake" every day.

4.  Sales space is valuable. You may want to charge every product in your line a certain amount of rent based on the space it takes up. Mail order catalogs do this with the space each product takes on a page. Every dead item in your store is taking up space that could be filled by a hot item.

5.  Turn lemons into lemonade. Many consumers are on the lookout for a bargain. Instead of slowly selling your "dogs" to

customers who are willing to pay full price, put up a window banner announcing your "drastic, inventory reduction sale." You may pull in customers who would have otherwise not purchased a bike at all, or bought their new two wheeler from a discount house.

6. Only rarely should you attempt to return product to your supplier. Usually, you are in a better position than he is to move the item. He may be sitting on a mountain of it, and you will only add to his problem. Your insistence on returning good quality merchandise that is merely "not stylin'" will hurt your relationship with the vendor and potentially hurt his future ability to serve you.

   However, if you aren't particularly mindful whether you have a future with the supplier, and/or if keeping the product may result in serious damage to your ability to continue in business, by all means, use all necessary pressure to exact an agreement to return the merchandise.

## IN STOCK

You've really done your homework. The bicycle lines you have selected for next year are "dyn-o-mite." You are totally confident that you have carefully measured each bike against what you hear your customers requesting.

The season opens, and you hit the bull's eye. You're having the best Spring in your history. In fact, business is so good, you need another 100 bicycles, and you need them fast. No sweat. Your sales rep, Jim, will be thrilled to get this surprise.

Turns out Jim has been getting surprises all this week. His fellow reps across the country have also started planning their retirement based on the bonuses they're going to earn from all these orders. Jim's voice falters as he speaks the unspeakable: "Out of stock." How can you avoid this?

An important part of your line selection includes supplier reliability. Is this vendor likely to have the resources to back up its dealers? Will they be willing to take the necessary risk on inventory so that you don't have to bear it all? Do they have the clout with the component suppliers to get scarce parts when shortages develop?

Carry several lines of bicycles. It is the rare dealer today who only carries only one or two brands of bicycles. There are advantages to buying fewer lines, but buying them in depth is the key. However, the fewer lines you plan to buy, the more critical it is that each supplier is prepared to back you up.

## IN SUPPORT

How much advertising will the distributor do at all levels? Is there a co-op advertising plan for the dealer? What about team sponsorship, other public relations efforts, and in store merchandising aids?

What kind of territory will you have? What kind of dating is offered? What other services are offered such as training, seminars, manuals, videos, or other demo materials?

Who pays the freight? Are the recommended retail prices advertised? If so, what are the margins? Are there volume discounts?

## IN DOLLARS AND CENTS

I purposely left the cost issue until last, even while touching on it in the last paragraph. What you pay for something is VERY important. However, a great price on an item that doesn't sell, hurts your image. If it is out of stock just when you need it, is worthless. **Establish the above criteria first, then argue about the price.**

When it comes to this sensitive issue, it seems appropriate to begin by discrediting two prevailing myths.

Myth #1: *As a purchasing agent, it is my duty to beat the supplier out of his last nickel.*

Myth #2: *My supplier doesn't offer discounts, or might get mad if I ask, or I might hurt his survivability if I beat him out of a discount.*

All contracts are negotiated. The purchase order for bicycles is a contract. Two intelligent negotiators who intend to have a long-term relationship will attempt to 1) Negotiate in good faith; and 2) Arrive at a WIN/WIN agreement. If you are following these two criteria, and you believe that your sales rep is not, this should be a red flag warning about continuing to do business with that supplier.

In other words, if you are trying to extract the last possible nickel from you supplier merely to feather your own nest, and without regard for his needs, you should correct your thinking. However, if the seller seems disinterested in your real needs concerning competition, overhead, or current financial status, you may want to reconsider your plans to purchase from that source.

When it comes to the actual cost of any product you purchase, your interest should be in knowing with certainty that you are getting the same or better price as others similarly situated. It has always impressed me when a wholesaler says that **the price list is the price list,** and there are no deviations. On the other hand, I worry when I must negotiate every line item. This tells me that a better negotiator (with whom I may be competing) could be getting a better price from the same supplier than I am.

## IN SPECIAL CIRCUMSTANCES

There are many situations where it may be possible to make a lot more profit on the buy than on the sell. You should spend almost as much time and energy on these efforts as you do on building traffic. For while it is true that a well stocked store with no customers isn't going to produce much benefit to the owner, you cannot sell from an empty basket, either.

1. Distressed suppliers. If it is at all possible, keep near at hand a substantial amount of cash or credit. Hardly a week goes by that someone in our industry isn't experiencing a special need. They may have overbought (or undersold). They might have a bank loan due, or other large cash need. For any of a host of reasons, they may be on the verge of folding their tent.

   While I wouldn't want to have the reputation of encouraging

folks to become scavengers, the reality is that sometimes another's misfortune can help you build your fortune. And, importantly, **YOU WILL BE HELPING THEM, NOT HURTING THEM!!!** That comment takes us back, again, to the fact that contracts are negotiated by two intelligent persons. If someone is trying to sell an item for a ridiculous price, it's because they have a need for cash that is greater than their need for profit. FILL THEIR NEED.

Try to become a customer of every US supplier. Even if you only buy $50 a year from some of those that are far away. By receiving their monthly flier and other advertising pieces, you can keep abreast of these kinds of opportunities.

You may even wish to let distant suppliers know that you are primarily interested in "special opportunities." Almost every company likes to keep a list of those who are ready to "bail them out" when needed.

2.  Distressed dealers. According to one statistic, almost one in seven bicycle shops will close each year. Therefore, if you have six competing shops in your area, some time each year you will have an opportunity to help a fellow dealer go get a paying job.

    If you are in a large metropolitan area, you may be able to help several unfortunates each year. Ask your reps to keep you informed of situations they hear about. A recent questionnaire circulated by *Bicycle Dealer Showcase* to the BDS top 100 dealers indicated that one of the things they didn't care for about reps was the amount of rumor passing they do. Since reps will pass rumors, you can take advantage of, instead of being annoyed by, that tendency.

3.  Special promotions. If you are planning a big sale, use that fact to elicit special favors. Talk to your suppliers about deep discounts, consignment, advertising money, in-shop attendance by reps or factory demonstrators, display materials, video and video equipment. Any way they can help your sales, don't hesitate to ask.

    If your primary vendors don't seem to be too creative in helping you get hot specials on the best selling items, talk to some of the manufacturers, themselves. See if you can get them to agree to special help for your event. Now call your wholesaler back and tell him what the manufacturer has agreed to.

All of these special purchases have to be carefully analyzed. It doesn't do you much good to save 30% on an item and then sit on it for two years. However a 50% discount might make a two-year turnover acceptable. You can then consider whether to charge full retail and sell off the product over the long term, or use the item as a promotion while retaining full margins.

## IN CONCLUSION

In earlier writings I heavily promoted the fact that dealer needed a full 35% margin on bicycles after all real costs (the unit itself plus freight and assembly). Because of the increase in the variety of bicycle styles, colors, and brands, and because of the continuing escalation in the cost of overhead, I would now recommend that dealers seek a 40% real margin on all bicycles under $400 and on all specialty (low volume) bikes, regardless of retail price point. For those in competitive areas, it is unlikely that it will be possible to do better than 35% on high volume two-wheelers in the $400-$1,500 range, and in many cases that will be too much.

# CHAPTER 10

# STORE LAYOUT AND DESIGN

## Lean, Mean, and CLEAN

Some may find it odd that I start with this subject. It seems so basic . . . so common sense . . . too unlikely to provide new insight. RIGHT, **RIGHT,** and *RIGHT!*

Unfortunately, I can take you to shops from coast to coast which, regardless of the sophistication of their façade, window display, store layout, or use of fixtures, they don't even bother to sweep the floors daily.

Disney and McDonald's have built empires around this simple concept. Numerous articles have been written about it, but the other fast food outlets and amusement parks don't get it. People prefer to spend their money and are more likely to revisit businesses that are **CLEAN.**

Think about your own feelings when you are in someone else's retail store. If you walk into a retail establishment that is dirty, sloppy, or disheveled, don't you immediately consider that their products and services may be similarly dirty, sloppy, and of less quality than they should be. Sure you do, and for good reason.

So here are some basic, basic rules:

1.  Sweep, mop, dust, and clean glass displays daily. More often if necessary.

2.  Clean your rest rooms, dressing rooms, and counter tops daily.

3.  If the sidewalk in front of your store tends to collect debris, clean

it at least daily.

4. Completely dust and clean any window displays at least weekly.

5. Restock and straighten shelves every morning or evening.

6. Dust and wipe fingerprints off bicycles as needed. The best shops do this daily, as well.

7. Paint and restore interior walls, fixtures, storefront, and <u>signs</u> at least once per year. Major painting should be done every three to five years, depending upon climate and other considerations, but keep everything touched up at least annually.

8. Insist that all your employees dress neatly, in clean, respectable apparel. It is not appropriate to wear ripped clothes, halters, or sloppy looking clothing, regardless of style trends. Enforce a strict dress code.

9. Employee dress should include other aspects of appearance. You don't want ANY of your customers to have ANY excuse to leave or not return. Don't worry about being modern in the eyes of your employees. Worry about being sensitive to the needs and prejudices of your customers.

   Clearly this admonition does not include issues of sex or race. It is unfortunate if a customer refuses to trade with us because of the race or sex of one or more of our people. However, it is inappropriate <u>and</u> illegal to let these issues cloud our decisions.

   Your employees should understand that their jobs depend on your success. If something which they have control over, such as dress, might send a customer away, they should be just as interested in changing to more appropriate attire as you are.

10. Post a clear sign indicating your status as OPEN or CLOSED and what your business hours are. KEEP IT CURRENT. Keep it clean.

## Signs and the Times

A dealer friend of mine was contemplating spending $10,000 on a sign. He was concerned about laying out this much money "for a lousy sign." I told him it was only a lot of money if it WAS a lousy sign. An excellent sign that costs you only $3 per day for 10 years could be the best investment you ever made.

As one city after another increases the restrictions on retail store signage, it is getting harder and harder to have any impact with your sign.

However, the time and effort you put into this decision could have a major impact on your store's traffic . . . and therefore its success.

Symbols are easier and faster to identify than words. Thus you have the Union 76 ball, the McDonald's arches, and the Honda "H." It is beyond me why our industry has not developed a standard sign with a symbol that would be recognized nationwide. The NBDA has been trying. It would also allow a sign maker to create hundreds of such signs which would dramatically decrease the cost when compared to the one at a time approach.

Until this shortcoming is remedied, however, every bicycle store sign should include, at the very least, a neon, or three dimensional, or at least a colorful *bicycle*. I know this idea seems a little far out, but . . .

I know that you have a clever name for your store, or maybe you named it after yourself. However, the fact that you sell bicycles is FAR more important than the information that Jim is the owner or that the store is located in West Village. Even if you do have a clever name for the store, unless bicycle or bike is a part of it, make the name small and with a picture. I have a preference for highwheelers as an image and/or the word "bicycle" as big as possible.

Pay the extra necessary for a lighted sign, and then put it on a timer so that it is lit during high traffic times. Also illuminate your store window and interior to produce the greatest opportunity to have potential customers realize you exist. Lighting your store at night is also considered to be good burglary prevention, as it means the thief will be working in a spotlight.

In determining the placement, color, size, and other aspects of your sign, copy something you like. Drive around various business districts and look at other signs. See which ones attract your attention. Keep in mind that what is a good attention getter for a strip mall location may not work too well in a self-standing store.

Finally, create the largest, most visible sign possible within the confines of available space and local codes. Remember, either your sign or your Yellow Page ad is usually going to create the first impression your customer gets of your store.

## Window Wonderland

Take as many bicycles as you can, line them up in close formation and stick them in the window. This will surely let the world know you're in the bicycle business. It will also be boring and a useless waste of prime, and inexpensive advertising space.

Your window should be an opportunity to sell those who aren't thinking about a new bicycle or riding their old one. It should attract the attention of those who never even noticed there was a bike store on the block. It can also provide the consumer with an image of your business approach and what is new and exciting in bicycling.

While there are many ways to create exciting window treatments, my bias is towards the enclosed, theatrical approach. My attention is really drawn to the windows on many department stores where dramatic color, lighting, and display of product provide a desire to own "one of those."

The best displays of this type incorporate mood-setting dioramas. I can picture huge boulders sitting in front of a painted backdrop of a luscious forest on a sun-baked day. Two mountain bikes are descending through these boulders, and are propped in such a way as to suggest movement. For extra (although admittedly expensive) effect, the bikes are ridden by two attractive mannequins, clothed in the latest bikewear and wearing great looking helmets. The bikes are fully accessorized with color coordinated equipment. A high tech sign says it all - "Isn't this better than

Nintendo?"

Some stores are not that well-suited to enclosed displays. Certainly I don't recommend them where they will cut off all outside lighting. Interiors generally look far more vibrant with lots of sunlight.

In those situations consider hanging one or two beautifully detailed bicycles in the window. Again, angle these so that motion is implied. Consider having a window artist create a little background around the bike to add interest and vitality. For this type of treatment and the one above, price information should be kept tastefully at a minimum. However, there is nothing wrong with having one window of the store done in this manner while another uses the "INVENTORY REDUCTION SALE" approach.

If you are out of ideas, at least have a window artist create some starbursts and other graphics to let customers know what hot special you have right now. These don't all have to be about price reductions. Customers are also interested to know about brands you carry, new products now available, and special terms such as layaway or no payments until January.

Whatever types of treatment you use, be sure to change it at least once each season. Some may want to change their windows once a month to suit the special aspect of that month.

Take advantage of these selling days. A bicycle is a very romantic gift and surely deserves to be considered for Valentine's Day. It is a wonderful idea for Mother's and Father's Day or June grads. A two-wheeler is a fairly obvious back-to-school item, but I know of very few stores who put up a special window during that time of selling opportunity.

May is bicycle month. How many other products have a month devoted to them that gets national media attention? Do you take advantage by telling the story in your window?

Should you use a decorator? This will depend on many factors, not the least of which is how good you or your staff are at that type of thing. It isn't very expensive to hire a professional for this type of work. A major benefit is knowing it will get done, and that it will be changed periodically to maintain interest. Most well-run shops will use professional window dressers by the end of the '90s.

Last thought. Occasionally, especially if sales are a little soft, and if your image isn't so hifalutin' that you would feel uncomfortable doing so, create a wild and outrageous window. Rent a stuffed gorilla to ride a bike in your window. Have the entire thing painted like a mural with a bicycle theme. For Valentine's Day, let the neighborhood kids paint their initials in your window with "Jim loves Suzy" and "RK+PK=Love" using water-based inks.

If you take this approach, be sure to tell the local paper about it. They may do a photo story. An inch of type in the paper is worth twenty inches of ads. A photo story is ten times better yet.

## Superior Interiors

Have you ever eaten at a *very* fancy restaurant? You know the type. Where in addition to creating the best possible culinary experience, the food itself is presented like a work of art. The fact is it makes the food taste better. In addition, it allows the restaurant owner to charge far more than he otherwise could for that same food, and thereby work on much greater margins.

The same is true for the interior of your store. The minute a customer walks in he or she will be affected by the mood of the store. This could range from wondering whether it would be a good idea not to touch anything for fear of soiling their clothes to excitement at the prospects of their purchasing experience.

You would be surprised how inexpensive it is to move your store well up the ladder to the point where the customer will be truly energized by the environment.

You may wish to consult an outside professional for help in creating the perfect atmosphere. However, by visiting other retailers who have created the kind of mood you would like, you should be able to borrow their ideas without much trouble or expense.

Most of the drama is created by the color and material of floor and wall coverings, the proper use of lighting, incorporation of mirrors to create illusions such as size, and effective use of displays and merchandisers.

What kind of look will your customer be impressed with in the last few years of the '90s? It surely will not be glitz and glamour. I feel that most consumers will be looking for a family atmosphere.

The family will reign supreme for the next ten or more years. Your average customer will again have two kids under fifteen. Many more of your customers will be in their forties. These two facts can be easily culled from population data.

As the baby boom ages and the echo boom moves into its teens, parents are leaning toward a return to wholesome living. Drinking is down. Credit use is way down. Savings are up. Family movies are making a comeback. And, if all this isn't proof enough, politicians are all vying to see who is the biggest champion of the family.

Therefore, you may want your interior to reflect this change. Brick facades or wood paneling. Medium lighting, neither too harsh nor too soft. Even a fake fireplace may not be going too far.

It will also mean the end of posters with scantily-clothed women. Replace these with pictures of families cycling together.

It was never appropriate but hard rock music blast-ing away will also be a turn-off for these customers. The generation that brought us psychedelic colors, hippies, and drugs is yearning for a return to the simpler life of the fifties. You could even use that as a theme.

Of course, you may feel that your specific customer base will have a completely different attitude than the one outlined above. If you are catering primarily to a university crowd, you will probably want to keep an ear to the ground for trends in color and what's hot and what's not.

General Layout - If a customer comes into your store looking for a bike, he will find it. It isn't necessary to place the bicycles at the front of the store to accomplish this.

Like a grocery store who puts the milk in the back so you have to go past all kinds of other tantalizing products to pick up a gallon of 2% whole; or the department store that knows you didn't come in looking for perfume so they feature perfume and make-up at the door; you can greatly increase your accessory and clothing sales by placing these in the highest traffic areas.

If service is an important part of your image, make it very visible. However, this will mean that it should also be totally neat and well organized at all times. If you are not so concerned about repairs, and showing the service area will detract from the mood you are trying to create, don't hesitate to seal it off as much as possible.

I favor a second door for bringing in repairs. It doesn't help you in your effort to keep the store clean if customers are dragging dirty repair bikes across your rug all day. However, if it isn't possible to create a second entrance, consider using tile instead of carpet as a floor covering. At the very least, create a tile pathway from the door to the service entrance with carpet on either side for your display area.

Put your cash register in the front. It reduces shoplifting, and gives you a much better view of the entire enterprise when you must handle checkout. If possible, hire someone to handle the cash register full time or at least in the afternoon and on Saturday. This allows sales personnel to get on to the next sale.

Displaying Bicycles - It does nothing to increase a customer's awareness of the scope of his choices to display 300 bicycles in a 1,200 square foot area. It is far more effective to select 10 or 15 bikes and show them off one at a time in their best light.

For maximum effect, construct a display unit which has a backdrop. Use the backdrop to list features and benefits. The written word carries much more weight with consumers than anything you can say to them. Pretty ironic since you will have been the one to create the written information.

For some shops, you have no choice but to "store" as well as display all of your bicycles in the showroom. However, if you have a choice, limit the number of bicycles on display to the number that can be effectively used to make a presentation.

Displaying accessories - The end of the nineties will also see the end of packaging that requires plastic as the "Green" movement holds increasing sway over things political. There will also be a general reduction in the overall use of any kind of packaging. This will leave you with two possible alternatives for displaying accessories: return to the days when everything was under glass; or develop new displaying techniques using bins and shelves.

Manufacturers, including AC International, are already moving to change their packaging (We changed the Mr. Tuffy packaging to eliminate plastic and to maximize use of recyclable materials.) This is a time when bicycle shops can be the wave of the future, and actually derive a benefit against the mass market. It will be far easier for a small retailer to switch to the new displaying approach than for the Wal-Marts of the world. This will mean that the earth-conscious consumer will be drawn to your shop if you are minimizing the use of packaging.

In making the switch, I certainly hope that for all but the most expensive or likely to be shoplifted items, you will choose to keep most of your accessories readily accessible to the customer. It took a long time to get the average dealer to overcome the fear of the shoplifter, but we have all enjoyed the extra sales benefits offered by taking product out of the display cabinet, and the much feared increase in shoplifting never materialized. This will be true for the new packaging approaches as well.

Start making the switch now. Create permanent displays for products that can be stored without packaging or that are available bulk. If the product is only available in an unacceptable package, but you have an idea of how to display it without the package, remove it from the package and recycle what you can.

Once you have begun this transformation, make a big deal about it. Put up signs on your front door and/or window. Create a brochure that tells about the "greening" of Abe's Cyclerama. Put it near your cash register, as part of your literature room or wall (see following), and in other strategic locations. You may even want to develop a press release on the subject.

The literature room or wall - An informed consumer is a better consumer. The more information you can get into the hands of your customers the more you will whet their appetite to increase their participation and therefore their purchasing for their pastime.

If you have the space, I would recommend the development of a separate "room" for a person to be able to browse over literature, brochures, magazines, tabloids, and books. This could also be a place to set up a video unit for customers to preview videos or view demo tapes. An important part of this department would be a bulletin board to announce upcoming events that the store is involved with. You might also allow community organizations to put up posters or announcements, and offer customers the chance to put up small ads for used bicycles.

If you can't devote an entire room to such a project, you may want to give it eight or ten feet of wall space. Dealers who took me up on this concept after proposing it in the 2nd edition of *Principles of Bicycle Retailing* have unanimously confirmed its benefits.

Use of Promotional Materials in the Store - There are huge amounts of valuable space in the average bicycle store going to waste. Through signs, displays, brochures, and the like, you should be able to increase your overall sales. These types of materials should be displayed on counter tops, especially near the check-out and repair receiving areas; attached to gondolas, racks, and other merchandisers; even hung from the ceiling.

It is possible to go too far with this type of thing, to the point where the store starts to look junky. However, I have have never seen a bicycle store where that was the case. Rather, I am often amazed to see the most valuable space in any retail environment going totally unused. Major mass merchants actually charge their suppliers rent to put merchandise near the cash register; yet many, if not most, bike shops don't even have a sign or brochure in the vicinity of check out.

Use Signs to Departmentalize - If the customer is in a hurry and you're busy, you want him to be able to find what he's looking for quickly and easily. There is very little that is more frustrating for a consumer than to enter unfamiliar territory and not be given any kind of map. You can create silent salesmen just by use of a few inexpensive signs.

Therefore, put like things together: helmets in one section, shoes in another; 20" bikes in one area, fitness equipment somewhere else. Now have professional signs created with large letters that designate each area.

## CHAPTER 11

# NO COMPUTER? — NO BUSINESS!

The computerization of the bicycle retailer to date has created three distinctly different conditions.

1. Many stores have very successfully added computers to their operation and reaped benefits in bookkeeping, sales and marketing analysis, and word processing/desktop publishing.

2. A larger group has attempted to computerize, and has totally wasted the investment, often hurting their business due to misallocation of time or money.

3. A very large segment have yet to invest in their first computer due to lack of knowledge, funds, or interest.

There has not been any type of survey taken, but there is a general sense among reps and others who follow such trends with a great deal of interest that those in the first group are very successful and getting more so. Those in the third category are holding their own. It is those described in number two that are in the biggest trouble.

It will be the goal of this chapter to save those in group two from allowing their electronic monsters to devour their otherwise successful enterprise. In addition, there will be a step-by-step guide for those who haven't stuck their toe in the water until now, to begin the process of entering the information age.

Some aspects of computerization are really quite easy. Other aspects are among the most difficult tasks in business. The most common mistake is not understanding which is which.

Shops selling over $200,000 per year, or who expect to or hope to, will need electronic assistance. Without it, they will be at a substantial competitive disadvantage. Chains of large, well managed, completely automated stores will be coming to every neighborhood where there is potential for sales of $200,000 or more. Their efforts will actually expand the overall market. However, it is unlikely that the unsophisticated bike store owner who still keeps his money in a tin box will be around to enjoy the increase.

## The Bike Store of the Future

The information age will not change the initial meeting with your customer very much. Selling is selling, and to the extent that you follow the methods outlined in this book, you can expect to close the same percentage of sales in 2001 as you do today.

There will be a few changes in the options available to the consumer, however. You will carry a much smaller inventory of bicycles and fitness equipment than you do today. You will carry more depth in your hottest sellers, and almost nothing in the less popular models, sizes, and colors.

When it comes time to determine the exact product for your customer, you will go to your computer, and look up your stock position on the item needed. If the item is not in your stock, it will be in your distributor's stock. Your computer will be able to instantly determine where you can get the out-of-stock item immediately.

Once the consumer has agreed to the special order, you will merely push a button and the order will be placed instantly in the distributor's computer. You will be able to note whether you wish it shipped that day, held for your normal weekly shipment, or held for will call.

As you ring up sales during the day, each item purchased will be noted by your computer system, as well as read by the supplier of that item on their computer. Once each week, your various suppliers will automatically replenish your stock of items sold. The distributor will either increase or decrease your stock levels depending upon historic sales data for each item as well as seasonal considerations.

When supplier salesmen call, they will carry or you will supply them with a hand-held computer inventory taker. They will count your inventory of items they sell you. This inventory will be automatically compared with the information in your computer and theirs. If there are differences between what the computer says should be on hand and what is actually counted, you can attempt to evaluate the reasons for each such discrepancy, and make changes accordingly.

The inventory print out will also suggest items that seem to be gathering dust. From this information you will be able to make decisions to mark down, change locations, or increase promotion.

At the end of each day or other reporting period, you will be able to see as much financial and marketing data you choose. You will even be able to program the computer to tell you only those things which are not in line with expectations. In other words, if you tell the computer to expect a 50% margin on accessories, and a 35% margin on bikes, and that this can vary from reporting period to reporting period by 10%, the computer will only tell you when you are more than 10% above or below those projections.

When you receive merchandise from a supplier, you will check the order in with a scanner. The scanned information will automatically compare what you have received with your purchase order. You will then automatically notify the supplier of any discrepancy or that the shipment was received as ordered. As soon as you have confirmed the receipt of product, the supplier's computer will enter an invoice for that amount, and electronically transmit the invoice to your computer.

When it comes time to pay bills, your computer will print out the bills it believes should be paid on any given day. If you agree, a single key stroke will result in your computer calling up the computer at the bank, which will in turn create electronic transfers of cash to your supplier and notify the supplier that the item has been paid.

Does all the above seem like so much science fiction? Guess again! Everything described above is already happening somewhere in the retail environment. The most sophisticated and fastest growing mass marketers such as Wal Mart are incorporating almost every idea above . . . RIGHT NOW! It's all a part of the new EDI (Electronic Data Interface) system. Does it now begin to become clear why these retailers are able to work on much smaller margins than you are?

## What Computers Can/Can't Do For You Today

If, after reading the above, you still believe you can be competitive without entering the computer age, take a look below at what a computer can do for you, RIGHT NOW.

1. Take the place of a typewriter.
2. Act as a fax machine.
3. Become a telephone answering machine and voice mail system.
4. Create professional brochures, mailing pieces, price lists, advertisements, newsletters, and forms.
5. Construct data bases of information that will allow you to better understand your customers, review product options, and make personalized mailings to your customers.
6. Develop spread sheets to formulate projections of sales, earnings, cash flow, budgets or purchases. Instantly see the effect of changes in any category over time.
7. Evaluate and control inventory.
8. Report sales by product, category, customer, supplier, or salesman.
9. Replace your cash register.
10. Produce automatic purchase orders.
11. Calculate payroll deductions and print out payroll checks.

12. Keep track of all accounts receivable and payable.
13. Store and integrate all other accounts, such as cash, notes, capital, deposits, and employee advances.
14. Create earning statements (profit and loss) by day, week, month quarter, year.
15. Provide complete financial statement for any period.
16. Act as a filing system.

I'm sure that a good computer salesman could come up with even more business applications. In addition, there are more lists of personal benefits available to you and your family. My two year old is learning his letters and numbers on ours, my fifteen year old writes her term papers with the same machine, and my wife uses a program called HyperBible to help her with Bible studies.

So far, my intention has been to make certain that every reader understands the necessity of bringing a computer into the business. The next section of this book should be read and re-read by those who are already computerized, but not having a pleasant experience, and by those who are ready to move forward into electronic systems.

## What a computer will not do for you:

1. It will not make you or your staff better salespeople.
2. It will not clean up the floor or wash your windows.
3. It will not restock your shelves.
4. It will not create a visually appealing store front or selling floor.
5. It will not come up with ways to bring more customers in the door.
6. It will not hire more competent help.
7. It will not pay the bills when you are out of money.

The computer does not make up for weaknesses in your organization. You must always keep the fundamentals of good management in the forefront. The computer is a tool that aids you in carrying out these fundamentals.

## MORE of what a computer will not do for you:

1.  It will not give you better information back than that which you put into it. The computer industry coined a term for this phenomenon at least twenty years ago.

## GIGO ... GARBAGE IN - GARBAGE OUT

If you are trying to use the equipment to keep track of inventory, and you forget to enter merchandise you receive from a vendor, your information is now flawed. If many      such transactions are not entered, the data becomes virtually worthless.

This is true for inventory, accounts payable, and ultimately, your Earning's statement.

2.  If you are not a good bookkeeper now, the computer will not make you one. If you don't know how to read a financial report now, you won't mysteriously learn how to because your computer creates it.

In other words, you or someone on your staff is going to have to be knowledgeable about the things you are asking the computer to do for you. This is true even if you are merely trying to use the machine as a typewriter. If you don't type well, it will still take you a long time to type a letter on a computer.

Such skills become even more critical for bookkeeping procedures. If you are always forgetting which one is a debit or a credit, you are not ready to use a computer for general ledger functions.

3.  A computer is a complex piece of equipment. Even the MacIntosh, which is by far the simplest to learn and operate, requires someone in the organization to become proficient at using the machine. A wheel truing stand is very simple by comparison, but it takes training and practice to use one. I firmly believe that the **owner** of any enterprise should try to know all about the workings of the company computer system.

In addition, you will be well advised to have competent, reliable suppliers who can back you up when there are hardware or software problems.

4. Computers do not immediately save you money or time. In fact, in the early stages a computer will cost you plenty of both. Long term, a fully integrated computer system may not add very much cost in equipment or labor, but it will add some.

The earn-out in using computers is the information they give us, the marketing methods that could not even been considered without them, and the potential for better management of almost every department.

## Selecting the Right System

Step one - If you are not already proficient in the use of a computer, purchase a simple unit and learn how they work. Most PC's today can use "Windows" software that is similar to MacIntosh. I would recommend that you either buy a Mac or a PC and "Windows." These are the easiest systems, and they are at least as sophisticated as "menu" type systems.

You may want to take a class, read books, or subscribe to magazines about computers. As with any other pursuit, the more you learn about these electronic marvels, the more benefits you will derive.

As a bare minimum, you will want to learn how to use the computer for a word processor (typewriter), data base (filing system), and spread sheet (data organizer). If you have artistic capabilities you might want to work with Pagemaker or other desktop publishing programs to develop advertisements, newsletters, or brochures.

Another major benefit of spending a few hundred hours with your own computer before entrusting your shop bookkeeping to automation is getting used to certain hazards that come with the territory. For instance, every operator has failed to save what they are working on, only to have the system "bomb" resulting in all unsaved data being lost. Far better that this lost data be a letter you were writing to your Mom rather than the week's receipts. Many other such learning curves await the new computer owner.

Step two - Work with your bookkeeper or CPA to establish good "hand" reporting systems for sales, inventory, purchasing, receiving, accounts payable, and cash. An established maxim of computers is that before automating these systems it is important that you have established the procedures and discipline of creating the data by hand.

Failure to establish working "hand" systems is probably the number one mistake made by businesses seeking to computerize. Computers are very unforgiving. An electronic error will commonly affect several different systems. For instance, if you were to record the sale of a helmet incorrectly by indicating six were sold rather than one, the computer would reduce inventory by six, increase the suggested quantity for your next purchase, and overstate your sales and profit.

In a "hand" system, it is very likely that your incorrect entry would have only been made once, since the sales slip, inventory card, purchase decision, and profit and loss are not all generated by a single key stroke, but by four separate entries.

As you develop good bookkeeping systems, you learn about the importance of checks and balances, accuracy, discipline, and paper flow. As in the example cited above, it is better to learn these skills when everything is on paper, than when it is stored electronically.

Step three - Once you have some basic computer knowledge and have established good bookkeeping procedures, you are ready to select a system and a vendor. **If you attempt to computerize without steps one and two, your odds of success are very limited.**

Before starting to call possible suppliers, consider what you would like the computer to do for you. Look over the list above for ideas. Consult with your accountant or other dealers who have already put in a system.

It is very common for retailers to begin with a system that only charts sales, records receiving of product, and keeps track of inventory. Through one-step P.O.S. (point of sale) systems or two-step systems that require keying in data separate from the transaction, many management reports can be generated.

You can determine gross profit by dollar volume or percentage of sale. You can see this by category or product line. You can generate suggested purchases, see sales trends by item or grouping, and keep track of your total inventory investment. Through such reporting you should be able to reduce your inventory, increase turns, and spot poor sellers earlier. These savings will help to offset hardware, software, and time investments.

For less than $4000 you should be able to buy the computer, software, and printer necessary to set up a two-step system. You will need very little outside vendor support to get started. However, you should personally oversee the installation, establish the procedures, and make certain that the entire program is successful.

With this arrangement, you continue to use your hand system, but instead of posting receipts to written ledgers, you post receipts in the computer. Thus each day you enter all sales information, all data relative to merchandise coming from suppliers, and returns and adjustments.

For between $7,000 and $15,000 you can get into a P.O.P. (Point of Purchase, also known as Point of Sale) system with at least one cash register. These are more complicated to learn than the two-step. Therefore a large part of the expense is for training and support from the supplier. The trade off quickly pays for itself, however, in savings of your time to set up the system and elimination of the posting of sales.

With a P.O.S., each sale you ring up automatically tells your computer that there is one less of that item, and how much the consumer paid for it.

Either one of these systems will already have the power and maybe even the software to do correspondence (word processing), newsletters (desktop publishing), brochures (various), and mass mailings of personalized letters (mail merge). However, you should determine prior to purchase which of these functions are important to you, and how much activity you will devote to each.

161

You may want more than this out of your computer. You may want it to create purchase orders, keep track of payables, generate payroll checks, and even provide an earnings statement. Very few independent retail stores are doing all of this, but if you feel so inclined, plan to spend $20,000 and significantly more time and energy bringing the system on-line.

After creating your wish list, it is time to call suppliers. **THIS IS GOING TO BE A SIGNIFICANT PURCHASE. THE INITIAL OUTLAY IS ONLY A FRACTION OF YOUR TOTAL EXPENSE. EXPECT TO INVEST A LARGE BLOCK OF TIME IN EVALUATING AND SELECTING A SYSTEM.**

I would propose that you plan to devote about fifty hours to the decision. This will include finding sources, interviewing suppliers, visiting existing installations to see potential systems in action, calling references, and negotiating the price and terms.

## Let's review these one at a time:

1. Finding sources. There are literally hundreds of packages and thousands of custom possibilities available. I would begin by reading the advertisements in bicycle industry publications. Next, call other bicycle retailers to see what they have purchased and how they like their system. Pick up a few issues of various compute magazines for other possible products. Network with other similar-sized retailers for their input. You may also get ideas from your accountant, banker, or local chamber of commerce.

2. Call as many of these potential sources as you can. Be prepared to give them a brief synopsis of your needs on the phone. Set up appointments with those who seem to have possibilities.

3. Interviewing suppliers. Make certain that the salesman presents you with a precise listing of what the computer can do for you, not just a list of parts and software. It is very common for computer suppliers to say their product can make diamonds

out of coal, when the reality is it can't even locate the coal.

4. Visiting installations. Insist on seeing at least two installations of any system you have an interest in. You can't learn enough from seeing the dummy installation in their showroom. You want to see a unit that has been operating for at least several months in a real world setting.

5. Think five times about purchasing any system from a supplier that can't provide you with almost endless references. Anybody can give you two or three. Ask for ten. Then ask for ten more.

6. Calling references. Most of what you want to know from existing users is pretty obvious. How do they like the system? What problems have they had? Was the computer powerful enough to handle routine tasks?

Less obvious, but far more critical in the computer purchase environment: What kind of service does the provider give? Do they get hardware fixes done within hours, as promised? Can you reach their software support people without calling dozens of times? Are the support people able to handle your questions? Has the salesperson continued to be available after the sale? Were there disagreements between you and the supplier as to what was promised versus what was delivered?

7. Negotiating price and terms. There is a lot of room for negotiating the price of a computer system. The sticker price isn't even close. The real number is probably about 20% off the first figure. Even after you think there is nothing left, it is often possible to get free software thrown in.

8. Make certain that your final payment to the supplier (not the leasing company) is made after the installation is 100% complete and you are totally satisfied with every aspect. It is common practice for the leasing company to pay for the system in full at the time that the physical hardware and software are installed. You should insist on progress payments with the last payment after all systems are up.

The danger in not following this advice has to do with a little clause in the lease agreement that amounts to a catch "22." The lease company isn't responsible for your happiness with the system.

Therefore you have to pay them, regardless of any foul ups. In the meantime, the supplier has no pressure to take care of you.

## Do's and Don'ts of Coming On-Line

DO walk before you run. Put in the various programs one at a time. Start with the one that can stand alone best. This would probably be your sales entry. Once you have confidence that this system is working perfectly, then add a second, say receiving. After that trial run, consider taking a complete inventory. At this point you will only be checking to make certain that your inventory is integrating with sales and receiving. You won't have to concern yourself with possible bugs in the two programs you have already perfected.

Once these are all running, you can add payables, purchase orders, etc. But, once again, one at a time.

DO take all the training yourself. Think carefully about the potential pitfalls of having a beautiful computerized retail business, but your expert gets sick or quits. You don't even know how to turn the thing on. You are in a real dilemma. Therefore, it is absolutely imperative that the owner know how the entire system works.

DO run parallel. As you tackle each phase of coming on line, continue to operate your hand system in addition to the electronic one for at least a month. Most serious glitches and hardware crashes happen early. In addition, the hand-prepared materials will allow you to check the computer's data to ensure accuracy.

DO listen to your experts. You have spent a great deal of time and money selecting the team that sold you your package. Do what they tell you to do. There will be plenty of times when you will be impatient or think you see a shortcut. Resist the temptation to innovate during the installation period. After you've been running successfully for awhile you can add or subtract from the basic program with less risk.

**DO** develop specific tasking. Specifically train individuals to be responsible for each aspect of your data processing. You may need to train everyone on the cash register, but limit the number of people who can enter receiving information, create purchase orders, etc. This is partially to increase the proficiency of each worker so assigned, but it is also to reduce the opportunity for fraud and embezzlement.

**DO** write down procedures. Each computer task should have a written procedure. No company goes long in today's world without turnover. You may be trained on every aspect of running the computer, but three years from now you may be a little rusty when Donna quits without notice. A written procedure will help you recall how to operate the program and be very useful in training the new operator.

**DO** pay attention to paper flow. One of the fastest ways to turn computer data into garbage is inadequate paper flow. Where does a packing slip go after the order is checked in? Is there a receiving document that shows if the packing slip and the actual account agree? How many copies are there of this receiving document? When the receiver is entered into the computer, where does the receiver go?

Every piece of paper created should have a clear path that it follows. As it winds its way along this path, it should create certain checks and balances to ensure accuracy and a paper trail for later audits.

**DON'T** turn over tasks to the computer that aren't cost effective. It is very easy to start turning over every possible job to your computer. However, many times it will actually take longer to use the computer for a certain function than it would to do so by hand.

Howard Sutherland of Sutherland's Bicycle Shop Aids offers a few examples:

1. Checking the computer to see if a certain bicycle is in stock during the course of a sale is no faster than looking it up using a card system. In addition, if you only have one terminal, you

may be interfering with other activity that needs to take place on the computer, or be standing in line to get access.

2.  Entering the customer's name, address, phone number, etc., at the time of sale. This may be O.K. when business is slow, but it can jam things up on a Saturday or other busy time.

3.  Accounts payable only makes sense if the store has thirty or forty suppliers, or if the intent is for a fully integrated accounting system. Otherwise it is much faster to do payables by hand.

DON'T forget about other management tasks. The computer can be hypnotizing. An owner can find himself spending lots of time trying to perfect various systems, while forgetting to sell, train others to sell, keep on top of industry trends, create strategies to increase traffic, and on and on. This is not a minor or unlikely problem, but one you should be very wary of.

DON'T become a hacker (computer addict). This is an individual who goes off the deep end. (Again, it isn't that unusual.) In this situation, the owner becomes consumed with buying the latest hardware, software, joining clubs, reading the hackers' publications, and completely ignores the day to day running of the business.

DON'T let the computer run your business. It's easy to be lulled into the idea that the computer is always right and always knows best. The management has to keep perspective and realize that the information being generated is no better than the interpretation by that management. Computers make errors, and those who put information and programs into computers make errors. If your gut feels funny about something the computer is suggesting, research the discrepancy.

There are plenty of potential pitfalls on the way to computerizing your business. However, the rewards are worth it, and the alternative (not computerizing) is not realistic. The other functions mentioned in the opening paragraphs of this chapter will be coming to the bicycle industry within years, not decades. The gap between the have's and the have-not's will greatly accelerate with the introduction of bar codes and systems that link customer and supplier, like EDI. The time to move is now!!

"I Don't Understand What Went Wrong
We Hit Our First Year Projection of $30,000
In Losses Right on the Nose!"

# CHAPTER 12

# BIKE SHOP PROFITABILITY

Over my years in the bicycle industry, I have met dealers with a range of attitudes about profits. The following examples are not meant to poke fun, but rather to wake some folks up to harsh reality.

The first group is made up of those who are in the business as a hobby. They like bikes, they like being around other people who like bikes, and they like the laid back style of the industry. The buy what they like. They open when they like. They are generally very happy individuals.

That happy disposition is commonly interrupted by an unhappy landlord, supplier, or banker. It turns to absolute doom and gloom as his home is foreclosed. A spouse who was happy with a mate whose business didn't interfere with family life, may not be quite so thrilled to find a lifetime of work and savings down the drain.

Then there are those who are very serious marketers and sellers. They like people, they are interested in selling people what they like, and they like the kind of people who buy bikes. They buy what their customers like. They are open during hours that their customers like. Their customers are very happy people.

Their customers are very disappointed to learn that their old friend who always gave them a break on the price, had every imaginable product in stock at all times, and was open from dawn till dusk, is having an auction to sell off the inventory and fixtures. The spouse left years ago and took the house and kids.

Finally, we have a group who likes business. They like the idea of owning a business, they like that people come to visit, and they like to make a good impression on these people. They buy what their suppliers like. They like to keep bankers' hours. They think they are happy.

Unfortunately, not enough people cared when the interior decorator came to reclaim the fixtures and furniture, and the supplier salesmen reclaimed their inventory. This owner was never married in the first place.

As the accountants, lawyers, and bankers poured over the losses from these three enterprises, one thing was apparent. None had ever taken an inventory, prepared an earnings' statement, or was familiar with a balance sheet. The first didn't care about those things, the second was too busy to take the time, and the third was going to hire an accountant next week.

If you do not understand the basics of accounting for profit, or if you are not clear on why margins matter, or if you have no idea about fixed and variable expenses, memorize the materials that follow.

Even the most sophisticated owners generally are not able to create a cash flow analysis. At the end of this chapter I will show you how to plan your cash for maximum return on investment.

## Basics

### The Sales Numbers

The information you want to gather from the paperwork surrounding the sale includes:

A. Total sales

B. Discounts, taxes, or other charges

C. A description of the item or service sold:

   1. For inventory purposes

   2. For sales analysis

   3. For future returns or warranty work

4. To determine commissions or compile results for sales contests

D. A sequentially numbered record of sales to ensure that all receipts have been accounted for

E. A record of cash or credit payments

Generally, you will be using either a cash register or sales slip to provide your customer with a record of the transaction. If you are not going to install a point of sale (POS) cash register that tracks the items you are selling, you should use sales slips. Otherwise, you have no way to record daily sales by item.

All sales should be posted to a sales journal. If you are not using a POS cash register or sales slips, there is very little to be gained in posting each transaction, so the gross sales total for each day is all you need.

If you are using sales slips, post each transaction to the sales journal. While doing so, post the quantity of each item sold in an inventory ledger. Also post any commissions or bonuses earned to an appropriate ledger.

If you allow customers to purchase from you on lay away or credit, you will also want to keep customer account cards where you can keep track of each payment.

Computerization of Sales information - The first thing that most companies will computerize is sales. The use of POS cash registers, or the computer posting of daily sales slips dramatically reduces the time involved in bookkeeping and dramatically increases the amount and use of data thus compiled. (See Chapter Eleven.)

## Accounting For Purchases

Many bicycle dealers fail to pay much attention to the purchasing and receiving side of their business. These owners are often quite diligent in seeking out customer thefts. Studies have repeatedly shown that more material is lost out the back door through employee theft and embezzlement than is ever lost due to shoplifting.

Additionally, suppliers can make mistakes in shipping and

invoicing. Others will shortchange you on purpose if you let them. Let's say you are purchasing helmets that normally sell for $40 on special for $35. Here are the things that can go wrong if you don't follow proper accounting steps.

1.  You don't count or check the helmets when you receive them. You ordered ten helmets at $35. You actually receive nine helmets of which two are a different style worth only $30. You have just lost the entire advantage of the special offer.

2.  The supplier of these helmets sends you an invoice for ten units at $36 and extends it to a total of $370. You pay the bill without checking it. You've lost another $20.

3.  You expect a $10 delivery charge. There is a $20 charge.

4.  You are offered a 2% discount if you pay within ten days. No where is this mentioned on the invoice. There is a note stating that if you do not pay within thirty days you will be charged 2% per month. No one pays any attention to this. You pay late and lose another 4%.

5.  Your buyer creates an order with instructions to ship the helmets to his home.

6.  Your bookkeeper tells you a bill must be paid by certified check. He takes the cash but never gets a certified check.

None of this needed to happen. There are methods of protecting yourself all along the way. Here is a simple system.

Begin by using purchase orders (PO's) for every order you or your buyer places. Even if you place the order over the phone, write up a formal PO and mail it to the supplier marked confirmation of phone order.

Include all the information about the purchase: Quantity, item number, description, price, extension, terms of payment, freight terms, tax, and any other charges, discounts or allowances. If there are later discrepancies, you have a document from which to make your case.

Your PO should have three or four parts. The original should go to the supplier. A second copy should go to receiving. A third copy goes to accounting.

**PO's should always be pre-numbered sequentially.** Whether the computer numbers the PO or the PO is pre-numbered, the buyer should keep a log of PO's. The log should show the date, PO number, and supplier. This control is important to the company and the purchasing agent. It shows that no purchase orders have been issued other than those in the log.

**You, the owner, should sign all PO's.** This protects you and the buyer against any misunderstandings in the future.

**All merchandise you receive should be accounted for on a receiver.** This document details any merchandise received by the company. The shipping clerk receives the ten helmets by UPS. Attached to the package is a packing slip. The shipping clerk counts the number of boxes received and the number and type of helmets received. There are blanks on the receiver for the shipping clerk to indicate number of boxes, quantity of product, and any discrepancies.

At this point the receiving clerk checks the packing slip to make certain that it agrees with his count. If there are discrepancies, he immediately notifies the trucker who has made the delivery and writes up any required documents.

The packing slip and bill of lading are attached to the receiver and the shipping department's copy of the purchase order. The shipping clerk should sign that he has received and counted the helmets.

Once the invoice arrives, the bookkeeper checks for any discrepancies and informs the supplier if any are found. If everything is in order, the assembled documents are filed for later payment.

When the bookkeeper gives you the check for your signature, it should be accompanied by the receiver and all attachments. This way, you have the opportunity to review the entire transaction if you like.

## The Income Statement

Many retailers "run their business out of the check book." If their bank account grows, great. If they run out of money, it's time to change something. Unfortunately for dealers who use this system, they are likely to find out too late that business doesn't work that way.

Rather, business is based on percentages. Using percentages helps you to determine why there is no money in the bank. It will also direct you to a possible solution. Here is a suggested income statement method for the typical bicycle dealer.

To understand the examples that follow, it is important to know the definition of the terms used.

Gross sales - The total amount of revenue from all sales of merchandise and services.

Cost Of Goods Sold (Or Services Delivered) - The total cost you have paid to make the goods or services in your gross sales ready for sale. For instance, the cost of the bicycle, any freight charges, and the labor to assem-ble it would all be part of cost of goods. In your service business it is the labor and overhead for the service area.

Gross Profit - Cost of goods subtracted from gross sales. If you buy ten bikes for a $100 a piece (cost of goods = $1000), and sell all ten for $150 each (gross sales = $1500), you are left with a gross profit of $500 ($1500 - $1000 = $500.)

Overhead - Everything else is overhead. Bookkeeping, general office, sales, advertising, and other such expenses fall into this category.

Fixed Overhead - Rent, office payroll, phone, depreciation of office equipment and furniture, postage, and office supplies are some of the items that represent the fixed overhead. They tend to stay the same regardless of sales.

Variable Overhead - Sales commissions and product liability insurance are examples of costs that are generally seen as a percentage of sales, rather than as a fixed dollar amount. These are generally also flexible. Advertising, promotions, and travel might be viewed as expenses that can be quickly cut or expanded, depending on specific circumstances.

Net Profit - Net sales minus all overhead. In our example above, you may have paid $100 to rent a space at the mall for the day, and a 10% commission to the salesman. Thus you would have had a total overhead of $250 ($100 in fixed overhead and $150 in variable.) This would leave you with a $250 profit for the day ($500 gross profit - $250 in total overhead.)

## Reading and Understanding Income Statements.

Here is the income statement of a very basic bike shop for one month.

| | | |
|---|---|---|
| **Gross sales** | $15000 | 100% |
| Cost of sales | 9000 | 60% |
| Gross Profit | 6000 | 40% |
| **Overhead** | | |
| **Variable** | | |
| advertising | 750 | 5% |
| commission | 450 | 3% |
| **Fixed** rent | 1500 | 10% |
| salary | 900 | 6% |
| phone | 600 | 4% |
| postage | 300 | 2% |
| **Total overhead** | 4500 | 30% |
| **Net Profit** | $1500 | 10% |

Each item is shown as a dollar amount. Then the amount is restated as a percentage of **gross sales**. (E.g., Salary is 6% of gross sales.) As sales change, it is interesting to watch the percentages change. In the following example, we see what might happen if sales doubled.

| | | | |
|---|---|---:|---:|
| **Gross sales** | | $30000 | 100% |
| Cost of sales | | 18000 | 60% |
| Gross Profit | | 12000 | 40% |
| **Overhead** | | | |
| **Variable** | | | |
| | advertising | 1500 | 5% |
| | commission | 900 | 3% |
| **Fixed** | rent | 1500 | 5% |
| | salary | 900 | 3% |
| | phone | 600 | 2% |
| | postage | 300 | 1% |
| **Total overhead** | | 5700 | 19% |
| **Net Profit** | | $6300 | 21% |

Overhead increased a few dollars but dropped dramatically in percentage of gross sales. This resulted in a substantial increase in profit.

Your income statement should be shown in more detail. In the bicycle business there is income from both sales of products and delivery of services. Therefore it makes sense to break out the sales from products on one line and the revenue from services on a separate line.

Other amounts are commonly subtracted from the gross income figure. Sales tax, discounts, returns, other credits are usually shown on the second line as these are amounts that reduce your gross revenue. When you give a discount on a bicycle, it is a good idea to show the suggested retail on the first line of the sales slip and the discount on the second line. When you account for this on your income statement you can track your average discounts.

Cost of goods becomes quite complicated. Let's say you had

$7,500 worth of inventory at the beginning of the month. You purchased $5,500 worth of product during the month (including freight and labor for assembly). You ended the month with $8000 worth of goods. Your cost of goods would be: Beginning inventory plus purchases less ending inventory or $7,500 +$5,500 -$8,000 = $4,500. If your product sales were $9,500, you would have a gross profit of $5,000.

Please note - all the above references are only to those items that you purchase and inventory for resale. When you buy a workbench or a computer, it is not included in "purchases" or in inventory.

Gross Profit - What kind of gross profit percentage (also referred to as margin) do you need?

| Landed cost of product | Margin percentage | Example | Retail | Real retail |
|---|---|---|---|---|
| under $1 | 75% | $.60 / 25% = | $2.40 | $2.49 |
| under $1 | 60% | $.90 / 40% = | $2.25 | $2.29 |
| $2 - $10 | 55% | $2.00 / 45% = | $4.44 | $4.79 |
| $2 - $10 | 50% | $9.00 / 50% = | $18.00 | $17.99 |
| $10 - $20 | 50% | $14 / 50% = | $28.00 | $27.95 |
| $10 - $20 | 45% | $17 / 55% = | $30.90 | $29.95 |
| $20 - $50 | 45% | $40 / 55% = | $72.72 | $72.50 |
| $20 - $50 | 40% | $45 / 60% = | $75.00 | $74.90 |
| **Clothing** | | | | |
| starting price | 66% | $5.00 / 33% = | $15.00 | $14.99 |
| sale price | 50% | $5.00 / 50% = | $10.00 | $9.99 |
| clearance | 33% | $5.00 / 66% = | $5.00 | $4.99 |
| **Bicycles** | | | | |
| under $200 | 40% | $200 / 60% = $333.00 | | $349.90 |
| over $200 | 35% | $300 / 65% = $462.00 | | $459.90 |

If you use the above approach, your goal after all discounts, returns, and shrinkage, would be a minimum of 40% gross margin. Better yet would be 45%.

## Profit Analysis for a Service Business

How do you figure your gross profit on service? In the simplest example, you are the sole service provider. Figure out how many hours per month you spend actually providing that service or in direct preparation for doing so.

Lets say you work 70 hours per week. Out of this, however, you spend 10 hours in administrative tasks having nothing to do with servicing bicycles. You spend 30 hours per week on the selling floor. Therefore you are spending 30 hours providing services. You are paying yourself $700 per week, for a total of 70 hours of work. An easy calculation shows you are earning $10 per hour. 30 hours X $10 means that your cost of service is $300. Your Cost of Service analysis would look like this.

| | | |
|---|---|---|
| **Gross Sales** | $900 | 100% |
| **Cost of Services** | 300 | 33.3 |
| | | |
| **Gross Profit** | $600 | 66.7 |

Since you are selling two or more very different kinds of products that result in dramatically different margins for each, you may wish to separate them on your statement. You should definitely separate your service profit analysis from your product sales.

Your statement for general and administrative expenses might look something like this (assuming $40,000 in sales):

**General and Administrative Expenses**

| | | | |
|---|---|---:|---:|
| Office Salaries | | 6600 | 16.50% |
| Payroll Taxes | | 660 | 1.65 |
| Rent | | 2500 | 6.25 |
| Utilities | | 700 | 1.75 |
| Interest | | 1100 | 2.75 |
| Travel | | 400 | 1.00 |
| Office Supplies | | 400 | 1.00 |
| Depreciation | | 1200 | 3.00 |
| Commissions | 6% | 2400 | |
| Advertising | 5% | 2000 | |
| Insurance | 1% | 400 | |
| | | ——— | |
| **Total General & Administrative** | | **18,300** | **44.90%** |

The next chart represents a real world bicycle retailer who sells bicycles, accessories, clothing, and service. This income statement will represent one month. The percentage figures are based on information from various sources, and may be much different than your store. Such things as rent can vary dramatically depending on location.

## Income Statement for ED'S FAMILY CYCLERY

| | | | |
|---|--:|--:|--:|
| TOTAL REVENUES | | 29,836 | |
| GROSS SALES (BICYCLES) | 14,455 | | 48.4%of total revenue |
| -Returns | 255 | | 1.8%of bike sales |
| -Discounts | 757 | | 5.2%of bike sales |
| NET SALES (BICYCLES) | 13,443 | | |
| COST OF SALES (BICYCLES) | | | |
| Beginning Inventory | | 28,350 | |
| +Purchases | 19,793 | | |
| +Freight In | 1,134 | | 5.7% of bike purchases |
| +Labor to Assemble | 540 | | 2.7% of bike purchases |
| -Ending Inventory | 41,522 | | |
| COST OF SALES (BICYCLES) | 8,295 | | |
| **GROSS PROFIT (BICYCLES)** | | **5,148** | 35.6% |
| GROSS SALES (ACCESSORIES) | 5,855 | | 19.6% of total revenue |
| -Returns | 87 | | 1.5% of access. sales |
| -Discounts | 66 | | 1.1% of access. sales |
| NET SALES (ACCESSORIES) | | 5,702 | |
| COST OF SALES (ACCESSORIES) | | | |
| Beginning Inventory | | 12,785 | |
| +Purchases | 2,775 | | |
| +Freight In | 112 | | 4.0% of access. prch. |
| -Ending Inventory | 13,045 | | |
| COST OF SALES (ACCESSORIES) | | 2,627 | |
| **GROSS PROFIT (ACCESSORIES** | | **3,075** | 52.5% of access. sales |
| GROSS SALES (CLOTHING) | | 3,756 | 12.6% of total revenue |
| -Returns | 153 | | 4.1% of clothng sales |
| -Discounts | 240 | | 6.4% of clothng sales |
| NET SALES (CLOTHING) | 3,363 | | |
| COST OF SALES (CLOTHING) | | | |
| Beginning Inventory | 9,507 | | |
| +Purchases | 650 | | |
| +Freight In | 0 | | 0.0% of clothing purch. |
| -Ending Inventory | 8,776 | | |
| COST OF SALES (CLOTHING) | 1,381 | | |
| **GROSS PROFIT (CLOTHING)** | | **1,982** | 52.8% of clothng sales |

| | | | |
|---|---|---|---|
| GROSS SALES (SERVICE) | | 5,770 | 19.3% of total revenue |
| COST OF SALES (SERVICE) | | | |
| Labor | 1,769 | | 30.7% of service sales |
| Overhead | 770 | | 13.3% of service sales |
| Materials | 140 | | 2.4% of service sales |
| COST OF SALES (SERVICE) | | 2,679 | |
| **GROSS PROFIT (SERVICE)** | | | **3,091**53.6% of service sales |
| **GROSS PROFIT** | | 13,296 | 44.6 of total revenue |

**OVERHEAD EXPENSES**

| | | | |
|---|---|---|---|
| -Payroll | 3,790 | | 12.7%of total revenue |
| -Payroll tax | 493 | | 1.7% |
| -Rent | 1,650 | | 5.5% |
| -Telephone | 225 | | 0.8% |
| -Utilities | 221 | | 0.7% |
| -Legal | 35 | | 0.1% |
| -Accounting | 75 | | 0.3% |
| -Depreciation | 120 | | 0.4% |
| -Advertising | 1,425 | | 4.8% |
| -Auto expense | 350 | | 1.2% |
| -Interest | 250 | | 0.8% |
| -Office expense | 275 | | 0.9% |
| -Commissions | 350 | | 1.2% |
| -Travel | 220 | | 0.7% |
| TOTAL OVERHEAD | | 9,479 | 31.8% |
| **NET PROFIT** | | **3,817** | 12.8% |
| **AFTER TAX PROFIT** | | **2,542** | 8.5% |

**NOTES:** The payroll figure may seem small. This is because much of the payroll is in labor to assemble bikes and in service labor. Some of the rent is also captured in the service overhead.

Some numbers are rounded off to the nearest dollar. All percentages are rounded off to the nearest tenth of a percent.

## Interpreting and Using Income Statements

The sample above shows a bicycle retailer who's doing everything right. If that was not apparent to you, hopefully it will be more so after reviewing the next example. This shop has several problems. Your assignment is to figure out why this shop is losing money and make some recommendations for returning it to profitability.

**Income Statement for BOB'S BIKE SHOP**

| | | | |
|---|---|---|---|
| TOTAL REVENUES | | **33,418** | |
| GROSS SALES (BICYCLES) | 14,985 | | 44.8% |
| of total revenu | | | |
| -Returns | 769 | | 5.1% of bike sales |
| -Discounts | 1,256 | | 8.4% of bike sales |
| NET SALES (BICYCLES) | | 12,960 | |
| COST OF SALES (BICYCLES) | | | |
| Beginning Inventory | | 28,350 | |
| +Purchases | 17,552 | | |
| +Freight In | 1,134 | | 6.5% of bike purch |
| +Labor to Assemble | 980 | | 5.6% of bike purch |
| -Ending Inventory | 39,325 | | |
| COST OF SALES (BICYCLES) | | 8,691 | |
| **GROSS PROFIT (BICYCLES)** | | **4,269** | 28.5% of bike sales |
| GROSS SALES (ACCESSORIES) | 6,355 | | 19.0% of total revenue |
| -Returns | 198 | | 3.1% of access. sales |
| -Discounts | 225 | | 3.5% of access. sales |
| NET SALES (ACCESSORIES) | | 5,932 | |
| COST OF SALES (ACCESSORIES) | | | |
| Beginning Inventory | | 15,532 | |
| +Purchases | 3,025 | | |
| +Freight In | 285 | | 9.4% of acces. purch. |
| -Ending Inventory | 15,642 | | |
| COST OF SALES (ACCESSORIES) | | 3,200 | |
| **GROSS PROFIT (ACCESSORIES** | | **2,732** | 43.0% of access. sales |
| GROSS SALES (CLOTHING) | 4,553 | | 13.6% of total revenue |
| -Returns | 325 | | 7.1% of clothng sales |
| -Discounts | 388 | | 8.5% of clothng sales |

182

| | | | |
|---|---|---|---|
| NET SALES (CLOTHING) | | 3,840 | |
| COST OF SALES (CLOTHING) | | | |
| Beginning Inventory | | 10,322 | |
| +Purchases | 1,050 | | |
| +Freight In | 130 | | 13%of clothng prch. |
| -Ending Inventory | 9,655 | | |
| COST OF SALES (CLOTHING) | | 1,847 | |
| **GROSS PROFIT (CLOTHING)** | | **1,993** | 43.8% of clothng sales |
| GROSS SALES (SERVICE) | | 7,525 | 22.5% of total revenue |
| COST OF SALES (SERVICE) | | | |
| Labor | 3,650 | | 48.5% of service sales |
| Overhead | 670 | | 8.9% of service sales |
| Materials | 170 | | 2.3% of service sales |
| COST OF SALES (SERVICE) | | 4,490 | |
| **GROSS PROFIT (SERVICE)** | | **3,035** | 40.3% of service sales |
| **GROSS PROFIT** | | **12,029** | 36.0% **of ttl revenue** |

**OVERHEAD EXPENSES**

| | | | | |
|---|---|---|---|---|
| -Payroll | 4,750 | | | 14.2% of total revenue |
| -Payroll tax | 617 | | | 1.8% |
| -Rent | 2,050 | | | 6.1% |
| -Telephone | 415 | | | 1.2% |
| -Utilities | 278 | | | 0.8% |
| -Legal | 35 | | | 0.1% |
| -Accounting | 75 | | | 0.2% |
| -Depreciation | 120 | | | 0.4% |
| -Advertising | 1,865 | | | 5.6% |
| -Auto expense | 400 | | | 1.2% |
| -Interest | 450 | | | 1.3% |
| -Office expense | 325 | | | 1.0% |
| -Commissions | 450 | | | 1.3% |
| -Travel | 220 | | | 0.7% |
| TOTAL OVERHEAD | | 12,051 | | 36.1% |
| **NET PROFIT** | | | **-22** | -0.1% |
| -Provision for tax | | 0 | | |
| **AFTER TAX PROFIT** | | | **-22** | -0.1% |

Hopefully, the problems of the second shop jumped right off the page at you. Let's take a look at some of the differences that resulted in a reasonable profit for one store and a loss for the other.

1. The first thing I notice is that Bob sold quite a bit more than Ed. As a sales and marketing kind of guy, I like that. A little deeper look, however, suggests that instead of great salesmanship, we might have great givesmanship. Ed's profit margin is lower in every area of sales. Ed says that if he could have enjoyed Bob's margins, he would have made a great profit. Bob thinks Ed wouldn't have enjoyed those extra sales without deep discounting.

2. Interestingly, Ed might have pulled out with a good profit after all, if it wasn't for a few other problems. It seems that his customers bring back a lot of stuff. It also costs him more to assemble a bike. He also pays too much for his service labor. These three together suggest he needs some better people in his service department.

3. Bob might also have some better purchasing and negotiating skills than ol' Ed. It would appear that Bob does far better on his freight. It isn't a lot of dollars, but even those few add up after a while.

4. Those extra sales had a couple of additional costs besides the lower margins. It takes more people to move more product, so the overall payroll increased. This also means more of Ed's time was spent in hiring, firing, and management, which either meant less time with the customers or with his family.

5. Ed also paid more for rent, advertising, and office expenses because of the higher sales volume. I suppose we'd all be happy to have those increases if we could depend on the extra volume. However, in many cases, Ed's percentage of total volume was higher, even though his volume was higher. This would suggest a need for better controls on these items.

6. There was one bright spot in all this. Ed didn't owe any income taxes.

## Make More Money - NOW!

Throughout this book I have proposed various methods for increasing your sales. Some involved increasing traffic through better advertising and promotion. Others involved selling more to those who visit. Yet another section made many suggestions of ways to sell to people who would never think to visit your place of business. It is my hope that you will try many of these ideas and greatly increase the volume of your store.

However, it is my further desire that you not end up like Ed. All that work and no income taxes to pay. So, in an effort to ward off that possibility, here are numerous proposals for making more profit, whatever your sales should be.

1. Once each week, walk through the entire sales area and look at every price. Wherever possible, raise the price: Bicycles, accessories, parts, clothing, shoes, rubber, service, everywhere. This exercise should be done judiciously, but take risks here and there. If there is too much resistance, or if you begin to sense that there is a general negative impression about your pricing, make quiet (or not so quiet) downward adjustments.

   It is very easy to allow margins to slip as you lower prices to meet the competition, but never test them again at higher levels. Some products have no price in the consumer's eyes and can stand substantially more mark-up than the average dealer gives them. Continuously evaluate and experiment.

2. Be aggressive in your buying. Get and read the classic book on negotiation, Herb Cohen's *You Can Negotiate Anything with Anybody*. There is a famous saying that more money is made on the buy side than on the sell side. This has to do with buying at the best price, and buying products that sell. Don't relegate your purchasing efforts to a "want list." Treat every buying opportunity as a profit opportunity.

3. Differentiate your product from the competition. Repackage product with your store name on it. Buy things bulk if brand isn't important, and create your own razzle dazzle with packaging or display. Try to locate products that aren't carried by

every other store in town. Only carry bike lines that guarantee you a certain territory. All of these approaches will allow you to charge much more than the other stores. You see, there is no competition for price between apples and oranges.

4. Get rid of marginal employees quickly. They are a drain on your resources. This is not to say that you should never attempt to develop someone. However, if you have someone who is not responding to your efforts to train them, move them out.

5. When an employee leaves for any reason, see if you can get along without that position. When you do re-hire, try to do so at a lower wage.

6. Train your employees. Retrain your employees. Review your employees. Set goals, standards, quotas, and performance criteria for your employees. Use motivational books, seminars, tapes, bonuses, contests, and commission to maximize each employees performance. Quantify and frequently evaluate your overall sales per employee ratio. Never let it go down.

7. At least once each quarter review every item on your income statement. Try to look at these expenses as if cutting them could be the difference between continuing in business and not. Is there any way to cut them?

Next, compare each one with your previous statements and with your expectations. Have any increased in dollars? In percentage? If yes, take a harder look at these. How has that happened? What can you do about it?

8. Could you save money by investing in automation, new equipment, having an energy audit, reviewing your phone bills, changing banks, or paying off a loan by lowering inventory, selling dead stock, or working out better terms with one or more major suppliers?

9. Do you have money in low interest savings vehicles that would be better invested in taking maximum discounts or anticipation? You might also be able to use sidelined cash to make special buys from cash short, inventory long suppliers.

# The Cash-Flow Analyzer

## Forecasting

Hopefully, each year since you started this enterprise you sat down to plan your revenues and expenditures for the coming year. A few of you have consistently developed five-year forecasts with the first year or two by month, and the rest by quarter. Finally, some of you are very serious planners who accompanied all of this with a cash-flow analysis and detailed notes for both. Those in the third group undoubtedly are doing very well.

When a company reaches maturity, one of the most important management tools it should develop is the fully annotated five year forecast.

The first compilation would be sources and amounts of revenue by type.

In other words, break your business up into as many components as there are businesses that depend on different customers, require different overheads, or produce different margins. As discussed above, at a bare minimum, you would divide bicycles, accessories, clothing, and service. If you carry non bicycle lines, this could add to your categories. You might even want to differentiate between brands of bikes or price ranges.

You might end up with a revenue plan that looks like this.

|  | 1993 actual | 1994 | 1995 | 1996 | 1997 | 1998 |
|---|---|---|---|---|---|---|
| New Bikes | 220,000 | 260,000 | 300,000 | 350,000 | 280,000 | 335,000 |
| Used Bikes | 20,000 | 25,000 | 35,000 | 45,000 | 45,000 | 45,000 |
| Accessories | 105,000 | 125,000 | 150,000 | 180,000 | 160,000 | 175,000 |
| Clothing | 77,000 | 95,000 | 125,000 | 145,000 | 120,000 | 140,000 |
| In Line Skates | 54,000 | 65,000 | 90,000 | 90,000 | 60,000 | 60,000 |
| Service | 75,000 | 75,000 | 70,000 | 70,000 | 80,000 | 80,000 |
| Total | 551,000 | 645,000 | 775,000 | 880,000 | 745,000 | 835,000 |

## Notes:

1.  Revenue from new bicycles will be emphasized. We would expect a continuation of historical sales increases due in part to unit sales increases and in part to inflationary forces.

2.  In any five year period we would expect at least one recessionary year. We have predicted that year as 1997. Experience suggests that we should expect to make up most of those sales in the following year.

3.  Used bike sales will be downplayed. We will primarily use this area as a way to sell off good trade-ins and to try to keep a customer who can't quite step up to a new bike. Though we will not seek to push sales up in this area, by selective buying and selling, we would plan to improve margins.

4.  Accessory sales should continue to grow at about the same rate as new bicycle sales. These sales will also be impacted by any recession, but not quite as much as new bikes.

5.  Clothing sales should also continue in an upward trend. However, the recession will impact this area more than any other, except skates.

6.  The forecast here is somewhat conservative as we have seen these fads come and go before. While this one looks more long lasting, it is very possible that sales will trail off.

7.  We have seen and expect to continue to see a decline in all types of service and parts due to improvements in bicycle quality. This will reverse slightly in recessionary years as people spend more to fix slightly older vehicles.

6.  All the above forecasted amounts assume an economy that continues to see GNP increases of 2.5% in expansion years and only experiences a recession of average length of twelve months, once every five years.

There are many other possibilities that would enter into the revenue source part of the equation. Do you foresee yourself adding an entirely new product or service line, opening a new shop, or developing a completely new brand? On the other side, are you likely to eliminate a marginal line, close a location, or pull back from a non-productive brand? Each of these should be considered in developing your sales forecast.

At this point, it is a fairly easy exercise to show the category by category cost of sales from the forecasted sales amounts to arrive at a gross profit for each. These are then summed up for a company-wide gross profit. As mentioned earlier, this line should also be shown as a percentage relative to total sales.

The hardest part to determine (at least in my experience) is what effect growth will have on general overhead. The simplistic approach would look at the historic percentage that overhead has exacted and apply that to the future. This seems right, but it just isn't so. In fact, overhead tends to follow a very specific pattern that is **anything but** a straight line.

Most of the time, as sales increase, overhead decreases as a percentage. This occurs for a time until you have maximized the efficiencies for a certain sales bracket. At a certain point you will see a dramatic increase in incremental overhead due to growth.

For example, we recently moved our business into a larger facility. If we have only a normal increase in sales, it will not make up the much larger rent, electric bill, maintenance cost, and moving expenses resulting from the relocation.

You can expect overhead to go up relative to sales with the addition of one or more managers, the addition and development of new lines, or the installation of new equipment (like computers). Of course, your overhead percentage is also likely to increase when sales go down during a recession or other short-term, unfavorable situation.

Having said all that, most of us believe our overhead should be trending down as a percentage of sales when our sales increase. But, how do you put a number on any of this? At what point do you project the addition of a bookkeeper, a sales manager, or a full time buyer? How do you predict when you will run out of space and need to add on or move? What will it really cost to knock out the wall and take over the space next door? (The rule of thumb is generally twice the highest amount you can possibly imagine. Though this comment may seem humorous, it is a fact.)

While it may not be easy to determine these numbers, you should take your best shot. Then include plenty of notes as to how you arrived at those numbers.

Having completed this exercise by year, for five years, you should next break down the first year, by month. Your bank or other financial backer might prefer to see two years by month. Through this exercise you will make certain evaluations as to seasonality (It is vastly different in Southern California than it is in Maine.) This will allow you to better evaluate your performance as the months go by, as well as help in the development of your cash flow analysis.

Your final forecast might look like this:

| | Jan | Feb | Mar | Apr | May | Jun | Jly | Aug |
|---|---|---|---|---|---|---|---|---|
| Sales - Bikes | 5,000 | 6,000 | 8,000 | 8,000 | 9,000 | 9,000 | 7,000 | 7,000 |
| Cost -Bikes | 2,500 | 3,000 | 4,000 | 4,000 | 4,500 | 4,500 | 3,500 | 3,500 |
| Sales - Accessories | 3,000 | 3,000 | 3,500 | 3,500 | 4,000 | 4,000 | 4,000 | 3,500 |
| Cost - Accessories | 1,950 | 1,950 | 2,275 | 2,275 | 2,600 | 2,600 | 2,600 | 2,275 |
| Sales - Service | 2,000 | 2,000 | 3,000 | 3,000 | 4,000 | 5,000 | 6,000 | 6,000 |
| Cost - Service | 1,600 | 1,600 | 2,400 | 2,400 | 3,200 | 4,000 | 4,800 | 4,800 |
| Gross Sales | 10,000 | 11,000 | 14,500 | 14,500 | 17,000 | 18,000 | 17,000 | 16,500 |
| less: rtrns & disc. | 200 | 220 | 290 | 290 | 340 | 360 | 340 | 330 |
| Net Sales | 9,800 | 10,780 | 14,210 | 14,210 | 16,660 | 17,640 | 16,660 | 16,170 |
| less:<br>Cost of goods | 6,050 | 6,550 | 8,675 | 8,675 | 10,300 | 11,100 | 10,900 | 10,575 |
| plus:<br>Other income | 800 | 800 | 800 | 800 | 800 | 800 | 800 | 800 |
| Gross Profit | 4,550 | 5,030 | 6,335 | 6,335 | 7,160 | 7,340 | 6,560 | 6,395 |
| less: general<br>overhead | 4,000 | 4,000 | 4,000 | 5,000 | 5,000 | 5,000 | 5,000 | 5,000 |
| Net profit | 550 | 1,030 | 2,335 | 1,335 | 2,160 | 2,340 | 1,560 | 1,395 |

| Sep | Oct | Nov | Dec | Ttl Yr 1 | Year 2 | Year 3 | Year 4 | Year 5 |
|---|---|---|---|---|---|---|---|---|
| 5,000 | 5,000 | 8,000 | 6,000 | 83,000 | 95,000 | 110,000 | 130,000 | 150,000 |
| 2,500 | 2,500 | 4,000 | 3,000 | 41,500 | 42,750 | 49,500 | 55,900 | 60,000 |
| 2,500 | 2,000 | 2,000 | 1,500 | 36,500 | 40,000 | 40,000 | 20,000 | 0 |
| 1,625 | 1,300 | 1,300 | 975 | 23,725 | 26,000 | 26,000 | 16,000 | 0 |
| 2,000 | 2,000 | 1,000 | 1,000 | 37,000 | 50,000 | 75,000 | 100,000 | 125,000 |
| 1,600 | 1,600 | 800 | 800 | 29,600 | 38,500 | 56,250 | 75,000 | 87,500 |
| | | | | | | | | |
| 9,500 | 9,000 | 11,000 | 8,500 | 156,500 | 185,000 | 225,000 | 250,000 | 275,000 |
| 190 | 180 | 220 | 170 | 3,130 | 3,700 | 4,500 | 5,000 | 5,500 |
| 9,310 | 8,820 | 10,780 | 8,330 | 153,370 | 181,300 | 220,500 | 245,000 | 269,500 |
| 5,725 | 5,400 | 6,100 | 4,775 | 94,825 | 107,250 | 131,750 | 146,900 | 147,500 |
| 800 | 800 | 800 | 800 | 9,600 | 12,000 | 15,000 | 18,000 | 21,000 |
| 4,385 | 4,220 | 5,480 | 4,355 | 68,145 | 86,050 | 103,750 | 116,100 | 143,000 |
| 4,000 | 4,000 | 4,000 | 4,000 | 53,000 | 58,000 | 72,000 | 96,000 | 108,000 |
| 385 | 220 | 1,480 | 355 | 15,145 | 28,050 | 31,750 | 20,100 | 35,000 |

As you examine this company's performance, test what you've learned.

Why did profits sag in year four when sales increased? If the other income consisted of rents from subletting unused space, do you think it is realistic to assume 100% occupancy, constantly escalating rents, and the continued availability of the space in the face of these sales increases? What other questions might you have about the above forecast?

## Cash-Flow Analysis

The spreadsheet approach that follows may be the single most useful tool available to the owner of a bike shop today. However, it is unlikely that even 1% use anything like it. You can do the following by hand, but the amount of work required is substantial. You can create this analysis on any spreadsheet program and have a quick and easy way to plan your company's cash future.

# The Assumptions

Before you can forecast anything about your business, you have to make certain assumptions. For the purposes of this example we will make the following assumptions:

Accounts Payable (A/P) - Payments will be made to vendors as follows: 20% will be paid within 30 days, 50% within 60 days, and 20% within 90 days.

Notes Payable (N/P) - An outstanding bank loan of $30,000 will be repaid at the rate of $1000 per month, plus interest of 1.25% on the outstanding balance.

Purchases - To maintain the inventory necessary to service customers properly, it is necessary to purchase the merchandise one month ahead of the need. Therefore, purchases reflect the replacement of merchandise sold in any given month plus the amount necessary to put in place the expected needs of the next month.

Operating expenses and commissions are paid in the same month as they are incurred. Commissions, returns, and discounts are shown as a constant percentage of total sales.

Payroll and benefits - Payroll will be seen as fixed except for the heaviest months of the year when extra help is predicted to be needed. Benefits (social security, workman's compensation insurance, and medical) are predicted to be 13% of payroll.

Other operating expenses are shown as specifically budgeted amounts.

In order for the spreadsheet to be complete, it is also necessary to know what the previous three month's sales were. We will say that these were for the just previous month, or month #1 = $40,000; the month before that, or month #2 = $30,000; and month #3 = $40,000.

We also need to know the forecast for the first month's sales of the following year. We will call this month +1 = 50,000.

The starting inventory, cash, and A/P would either already be known or be based on forecasts for previous periods. We have used figures that would make sense based on the other assumptions.

192

Cost of Goods Sold (COG) - The company will be assumed to have steady 45% profit margins. Therefore cost of goods sold will be 55% of sales.

## The Formulas

The basic cash flow formula will look like this:

---

Beginning Cash

+Net income

+Depreciation

+In<de>crease in A/P

+In<de>crease in N/P

Ending Cash

---

Therefore you begin with your cash-on-hand at the beginning of the period (month, quarter, year). You add to this the net income produced in the new period. (For this exercise, it will be month.) Since depreciation does not subtract from cash, you add this back in. If you increase your A/P, you have borrowed from your suppliers, thereby increasing your cash. Thus you will add any increase in this amount or subtract any decrease. Finally, you will add any new loans and subtract any repayments of principle.

The total of these amounts will provide you with your ending cash.

Next you need to determine the change in accounts payable (A/P). The formula will look like this:

Beginning A/P
> +Net Purchases
> -Discounts taken on payments (1%)
> -Payments
> > 20% of current purchases
> > 50% of purchases, month -1
> > 30% of purchases, month -2
> -Total Payments (sum of three above)

Ending A/P
In<de>crease in A/P (Ending A/P - Beginning A/P)

The brackets <> indicate that if there is a decrease, it is a negative number.
To find the change in notes payable (N/P):
Beginning Notes Payable
> -Repayments
> +Loan Proceeds

Ending Notes Payable
In<de>crease in N/P (Ending N/P - Beginning N/P)

The last formula is for Purchases:
Beginning Inventory
> -COG (55% current month)
> +55% of sales, month +1 (needed for next month's sales)

Ending Inventory
Change in Inventory (beginning Inventory - Ending Inventory)
Net Purchases (COG plus change in inventory)

By this formula, you have subtracted the amount of merchandise sold in the current month. Then you purchased enough inventory to replace the amount sold plus any increase or decrease in inventory needed as a result of the projection for the next month.

With these formulas in place, you can now construct the income statement. This will provide the rest of the pieces of the puzzle necessary to complete the cash flow analysis:

---

Gross sales
        -Discounts and Returns  (2%)
Net Sales
        -Cost of goods  (55%)
        -Commissions  (5%)
Gross Profit on sales
        +Other revenues
Gross Profit
        -Operating Expenses
                        Payroll
                        Benefits (13% payroll)
                        Rent
                        Maintenance and Repairs
                        Advertising and Promotion
                        Legal and Accounting
                        Travel
                        Depreciation
                        Interest  (1.2% End N/P)
                        Insurance
                        Utilities
        -Total Operating Expenses
Net Profit before taxes
        -Estimated Tax  (30% Net Profit)
Net Profit

---

With this accomplished it only remains to put all the formulas and the income statement onto a spreadsheet, project sales, insert known amounts (such as rent), and calculate.

| | JAN | FEB | MAR | APR | MAY | JUN | JUL | AUG | SEP | OCT | NOV | DEC | TOTAL |
|---|---|---|---|---|---|---|---|---|---|---|---|---|---|
| Gross sales | 30,000 | 40,000 | 50,000 | 40,000 | 30,000 | 50,000 | 60,000 | 70,000 | 80,000 | 30,000 | 40,000 | 40,000 | 560,000 |
| <Discounts and Returns - 2%> | 600 | 800 | 1,000 | 800 | 600 | 1,000 | 1,200 | 1,400 | 1,600 | 600 | 800 | 800 | 11,200 |
| Net Sales | 29,400 | 39,200 | 49,000 | 39,200 | 29,400 | 49,000 | 58,800 | 68,600 | 78,400 | 29,400 | 39,200 | 39,200 | 548,800 |
| <Cost of goods - 55%> | 16,500 | 22,000 | 27,500 | 22,000 | 16,500 | 27,500 | 33,000 | 38,500 | 44,000 | 16,500 | 22,000 | 22,000 | 308,000 |
| <Commissions - 5%> | 1,500 | 2,000 | 2,500 | 2,000 | 1,500 | 2,500 | 3,000 | 3,500 | 4,000 | 1,500 | 2,000 | 2,000 | 28,000 |
| Gross Profit on sales | 11,400 | 15,200 | 19,000 | 15,200 | 11,400 | 19,000 | 22,800 | 26,600 | 30,400 | 11,400 | 15,200 | 15,200 | 212,800 |
| Other revenues | 2,000 | 2,000 | 2,000 | 2,000 | 2,000 | 2,000 | 2,000 | 2,000 | 2,000 | 2,000 | 2,000 | 2,000 | 24,000 |
| Gross Profit | 13,400 | 17,200 | 21,000 | 17,200 | 13,400 | 21,000 | 24,800 | 28,600 | 32,400 | 13,400 | 17,200 | 17,200 | 236,800 |
| | | | | | | | | | | | | | 0 |
| Operating Expenses | | | | | | | | | | | | | 0 |
| Payroll | 7,500 | 7,500 | 7,500 | 7,500 | 7,500 | 7,500 | 7,500 | 7,500 | 7,500 | 7,500 | 6,000 | 6,000 | 87,000 |
| Benefits -13% payroll | 975 | 975 | 975 | 975 | 975 | 975 | 975 | 975 | 975 | 975 | 780 | 780 | 11,310 |
| Rent | 2,300 | 2,300 | 2,300 | 2,300 | 2,300 | 2,300 | 2,300 | 2,300 | 2,300 | 2,300 | 2,300 | 2,300 | 27,600 |
| Maintenance and Repairs | 250 | 250 | 250 | 250 | 250 | 250 | 250 | 250 | 250 | 250 | 250 | 250 | 3,000 |
| Advertising and Promotion | 2,000 | 2,000 | 4,000 | 2,000 | 2,000 | 4,000 | 6,000 | 6,000 | 6,000 | 2,000 | 2,000 | 2,000 | 40,000 |
| Legal and Accounting | 500 | 500 | 500 | 700 | 500 | 500 | 500 | 500 | 500 | 500 | 500 | 500 | 6,000 |
| Travel | 700 | 1,000 | 2,500 | 700 | 700 | 1,200 | 700 | 2,500 | 2,500 | 700 | 700 | 700 | 14,600 |
| Depreciation | 1,000 | 1,000 | 1,000 | 1,000 | 1,000 | 1,000 | 1,000 | 1,000 | 1,000 | 1,000 | 1,000 | 1,000 | 12,000 |
| Interest - 1.2% End N/P | 348 | 336 | 324 | 312 | 300 | 288 | 276 | 264 | 252 | 240 | 228 | 216 | 3,384 |
| Insurance | 700 | 700 | 700 | 700 | 700 | 700 | 700 | 700 | 700 | 700 | 700 | 700 | 8,400 |
| Utilities | 500 | 500 | 500 | 500 | 500 | 700 | 1,000 | 1,000 | 1,000 | 500 | 500 | 500 | 7,700 |
| Total Operating Expenses | 16,773 | 17,061 | 20,549 | 16,737 | 16,725 | 19,413 | 21,201 | 22,989 | 22,977 | 16,665 | 14,958 | 14,946 | 220,994 |
| Net Profit before taxes | -3,373 | 139 | 451 | 463 | -3,325 | 1,587 | 3,599 | 5,611 | 9,423 | -3,265 | 2,242 | 2,254 | 15,806 |
| Estimated Tax - 30% Net Profit | -1,012 | 42 | 135 | 139 | -997 | 476 | 1,080 | 1,683 | 2,827 | -979 | 673 | 676 | 4,742 |
| Net Profit | -2,361 | 97 | 316 | 324 | -2,327 | 1,111 | 2,519 | 3,928 | 6,596 | -2,285 | 1,569 | 1,578 | 11,064 |
| | | | | | | | | | | | | | |
| Beginning A/P | 40,000 | 42,911 | 47,686 | 44,689 | 38,413 | 45,360 | 52,807 | 58,532 | 64,203 | 43,484 | 39,376 | 40,822 | |
| Net Purchases | 22,000 | 27,500 | 22,000 | 16,500 | 27,500 | 33,000 | 38,500 | 44,000 | 16,500 | 22,000 | 22,000 | 27,500 | |
| <disc taken> - 1% payments | 189 | 225 | 247 | 225 | 203 | 253 | 324 | 379 | 368 | 258 | 203 | 231 | |
| <payments> | | | | | | | | | | | | | |
| 20% current purchases | 4,400 | 5,500 | 4,400 | 3,300 | 5,500 | 6,600 | 7,700 | 8,800 | 3,300 | 4,400 | 4,400 | 5,500 | |
| 50% month - 1 | 10,000 | 11,000 | 13,750 | 11,000 | 8,250 | 13,750 | 16,500 | 19,250 | 22,000 | 8,250 | 11,000 | 11,000 | |

| | | | | | | | | | | | | | Total |
|---|---|---|---|---|---|---|---|---|---|---|---|---|---|
| 30% month - 2 | 4,500 | 6,000 | 6,600 | 8,250 | 6,600 | 4,950 | 8,250 | 9,900 | 11,550 | 13,200 | 4,950 | 6,600 | |
| <total payments> | 18,900 | 22,500 | 24,750 | 22,550 | 20,350 | 25,300 | 32,450 | 37,950 | 36,850 | 25,850 | 20,350 | 23,100 | |
| Ending A/P | 42,911 | 47,686 | 44,689 | 38,413 | 45,360 | 52,807 | 58,532 | 64,203 | 43,484 | 39,376 | 40,822 | 44,991 | |
| Increase in A/P | 2,911 | 4,775 | -2,997 | -6,275 | 6,947 | 7,447 | 5,726 | 5,671 | -20,718 | -4,108 | 1,447 | 4,169 | |
| Beginning Inventory | 70,000 | 75,500 | 81,000 | 75,500 | 70,000 | 81,000 | 86,500 | 92,000 | 97,500 | 70,000 | 75,500 | 75,500 | |
| <Sales X 55%> | 16,500 | 22,000 | 27,500 | 22,000 | 16,500 | 27,530 | 33,000 | 38,500 | 44,000 | 16,500 | 22,000 | 22,000 | |
| Sales month +1 X 55% | 22,000 | 27,500 | 22,000 | 16,500 | 27,500 | 33,030 | 38,500 | 44,000 | 16,500 | 22,000 | 22,000 | 27,500 | |
| Ending Inventory | 75,500 | 81,000 | 75,500 | 70,000 | 81,000 | 86,530 | 92,000 | 97,500 | 70,000 | 75,500 | 75,500 | 81,000 | |
| Change in Inventory | 5,500 | 5,500 | -5,500 | -5,500 | 11,000 | 5,500 | 5,500 | 5,500 | -27,500 | 5,500 | 0 | 5,500 | |
| Net Purchases | 22,000 | 27,500 | 22,000 | 16,500 | 27,500 | 33,030 | 38,500 | 44,000 | 16,500 | 22,000 | 22,000 | 27,500 | |
| | | | | | | | | | | | | | |
| Beginning N/P | 30,000 | 29,000 | 28,000 | 27,000 | 26,000 | 25,000 | 24,000 | 23,000 | 22,000 | 21,000 | 20,000 | 19,000 | |
| <Repayments> | 1,000 | 1,000 | 1,000 | 1,000 | 1,000 | 1,000 | 1,000 | 1,000 | 1,000 | 1,000 | 1,000 | 1,000 | |
| Loan Proceeds | 0 | 0 | 0 | 0 | 0 | 0 | 0 | 0 | 0 | 0 | 0 | 0 | |
| Ending N/P | 29,000 | 28,000 | 27,000 | 26,000 | 25,000 | 24,000 | 23,000 | 22,000 | 21,000 | 20,000 | 19,000 | 18,000 | |
| In<de>crease in N/P | -1,000 | -1,000 | -1,000 | -1,000 | -1,000 | -1,000 | -1,000 | -1,000 | -1,000 | -1,000 | -1,000 | -1,000 | |
| | | | | | | | | | | | | | |
| Beginning Cash | 10,000 | 10,550 | 15,422 | 12,740 | 6,789 | 11,408 | 19,966 | 28,211 | 37,809 | 23,687 | 17,293 | 20,308 | |
| Net Income | -2,361 | 97 | 316 | 324 | -2,327 | 1,111 | 2,519 | 3,928 | 6,596 | -2,285 | 1,569 | 1,578 | 11,064 |
| Depreciation | 1,000 | 1,000 | 1,000 | 1,000 | 1,000 | 1,000 | 1,000 | 1,000 | 1,000 | 1,000 | 1,000 | 1,000 | 12,000 |
| In<de>crease in A/P | 2,911 | 4,775 | -2,997 | -6,275 | 6,947 | 7,447 | 5,726 | 5,671 | -20,718 | -4,108 | 1,447 | 4,169 | 4,991 |
| In<de>crease in Loans | -1,000 | -1,000 | -1,000 | -1,000 | -1,000 | -1,000 | -1,000 | -1,000 | -1,000 | -1,000 | -1,000 | -1,000 | -12,000 |
| Ending Cash | 10,550 | 15,422 | 12,740 | 6,789 | 11,408 | 19,966 | 28,211 | 37,809 | 23,687 | 17,293 | 20,308 | 26,055 | |

For this example we have used a marginally profitable business with fairly wide swings in monthly sales. You can see the effect that these sales changes have on cash. I have only shown four months of formulas, as the rest are replications.

| | JAN | FEB | MAR | APR | MAY |
|---|---|---|---|---|---|
| Gross sales | 30,000 | 30,000 | 40,0C0 | 50,000 | 30000 |
| <Discounts and Returns - 2%> | | =D3*.02 | =E3*.C2 | =F3*.02 | =H3*.02 |
| Net Sales | | =C3-D4 | =E3-E4 | =F3-F4 | =H3-H4 |
| <Cost of goods - 55%> | | =D3*.55 | =E3*.55 | =F3*.55 | =H3*.55 |
| <Commissions - 5%> | | =D3*.05 | =E3*.05 | =F3*.05 | =H3*.05 |
| Gross Profit on sales | | =D5-D6-D7 | =E5-E6-E7 | =F5-F6-F7 | =H5-H6-H7 |
| Other revenues | | 2000 | 2000 | 2000 | 2000 |
| Gross Profit | | =D8+D9 | =E8+E9 | =F8+F9 | =H8+H9 |
| | | | | | |
| Operating Expenses | | | | | |
| Payroll | | 7500 | 7500 | 7500 | 7500 |
| Benefits -13% payroll | | =D13*.13 | =E13*.13 | =F13*.13 | =H13*.13 |
| Rent | | 2300 | 2300 | 2300 | 2300 |
| Maintenance and Repairs | | 250 | 250 | 250 | 250 |
| Advertising and Promotion | | 2000 | 2000 | 4000 | 2000 |
| Legal and Accounting | | 500 | 500 | 500 | 500 |
| Travel | | 700 | 1000 | 2500 | 700 |
| Depreciation | | 1000 | 1000 | 1000 | 1000 |
| Interest - 1.2% End N/P | | =D50*.012 | =E50*.012 | =F50*.012 | =H50*.012 |
| Insurance | | 700 | 700 | 700 | 700 |
| Utilities | | 500 | 500 | 500 | 500 |
| Total Operating Expenses | | =Sum(D13:D23) | =Sum(E13:E23) | =Sum(F13:F23) | =Sum(H13:H23) |
| Net Profit before taxes | | =D10-D24 | =E10-E24 | =F10-F24 | =H10-H24 |
| Estimated Tax - 30% Net Profit | | =.3*D25 | =.3*E25 | =.3*F25 | =.3*H25 |
| Net Profit | | =D25-D26 | =E25-E26 | =F25-F26 | =H25-H26 |
| | | | | | |
| Beginning A/P | 40000 | =D37 | =E37 | =F37 | =G37 |
| Net Purchases | | =D45 | =E45 | =F45 | =H45 |
| <disc taken> - 1% payments | | =.01*D36 | =.01*E36 | =.01*F36 | =.01*H36 |
| <payments> | | | | | |

| | D | E | F | G | H |
|---|---|---|---|---|---|
| 20% current purchases | =.2*D30 | =.2*E30 | =.2*F30 | =.2*G30 | =.2*H30 |
| 50% month - 1 | =.5*20000 | =.5*D45 | =.5*E45 | =.5*F45 | =.5*G45 |
| 30% month - 2 | =.3*15000 | =.3*20000 | =.3*D45 | =.3*E45 | =.3*F45 |
| <total payments> | =Sum(D33:D35) | =Sum(E33:E35) | =Sum(F33:F35) | =Sum(G33:G35) | =Sum(H33:H35) |
| Ending A/P | =D29+D30-D31-D36 | =E29+E30-E31-E36 | =F29+F30-F31-F36 | =G29+G30-G31-G36 | =H29+H30-H31-H36 |
| Increase in A/P | =-(D29-D37) | =-(E29-E37) | =-(F29-F37) | =-(G29-G37) | =-(H29-H37) |
| | | | | | |
| Beginning Inventory | 70000 | =D43 | =E43 | =F43 | =G43 |
| <Sales X 55%> | =D3*.55 | =E3*.55 | =F3*.55 | =G3*.55 | =H3*.55 |
| Sales month +1 X 55% | =E3*.55 | =F3*.55 | =G3*.55 | =H3*.55 | =I3*.55 |
| Ending Inventory | =D40-D41+D42 | =E40-E41+E42 | =F40-F41+F42 | =G40-G41+G42 | =H40-H41+H42 |
| Change in Inventory | =D43-D40 | =E43-E40 | =F43-F40 | =G43-G40 | =H43-H40 |
| Net Purchases | =D41+D44 | =E41+E44 | =F41+F44 | =G41+G44 | =H41+H44 |
| | | | | | |
| Beginning N/P | 30000 | =D50 | =E50 | =F50 | =G50 |
| <Repayments> | 1000 | 1000 | 1000 | 1000 | 1000 |
| Loan Proceeds | 0 | 0 | 0 | 0 | 0 |
| Ending N/P | =D47-D48+D49 | =E47-E48+E49 | =F47-F48+F49 | =G47-G48+G49 | =H47-H48+H49 |
| In-de-crease in N/P | =-(D47-D50) | =-(E47-E50) | =-(F47-F50) | =-(G47-G50) | =-(H47-H50) |
| | | | | | |
| Beginning Cash | 10,000 | =D58 | =E58 | =F58 | =G58 |
| Net Income | =D27 | =E27 | =F27 | =G27 | =H27 |
| Depreciation | =D20 | =E20 | =F20 | =G20 | =H20 |
| In-de-crease in A/P | =D38 | =E38 | =F38 | =G38 | =H38 |
| In-de-crease in Loans | =D51 | =E51 | =F51 | =G51 | =H51 |
| Ending Cash | =Sum(D53:D57) | =Sum(E53:E57) | =Sum(F53:F57) | =Sum(G53:G57) | =Sum(H53:H57) |

199

Through the computer you can easily manipulate your forecasted items to see what effect will be derived by increasing or decreasing amounts or percentages. To get an idea of how useful this approach is, look at the next three, six-month forecasts to see the effects

| | JAN | FEB | MAR | APR | MAY | JUN | JUL | AUG | SEP | OCT | NOV | DEC | TOTAL |
|---|---|---|---|---|---|---|---|---|---|---|---|---|---|
| Gross sales | 20,000 | 30,000 | 40,000 | 30,000 | 20,000 | 40,000 | 50,000 | 60,000 | 70,000 | 20,000 | 30,000 | 30,000 | 440,000 |
| <Discounts and Returns - 2%> | 400 | 600 | 800 | 600 | 400 | 800 | 1,000 | 1,200 | 1,400 | 400 | 600 | 600 | 8,800 |
| Net Sales | 19,600 | 29,400 | 39,200 | 29,400 | 19,600 | 39,200 | 49,000 | 58,800 | 68,600 | 19,600 | 29,400 | 29,400 | 431,200 |
| <Cost of goods - 55%> | 11,000 | 16,500 | 22,000 | 16,500 | 11,000 | 22,000 | 27,500 | 33,000 | 38,500 | 11,000 | 16,500 | 16,500 | 242,000 |
| <Commissions - 5%> | 1,000 | 1,500 | 2,000 | 1,500 | 1,000 | 2,000 | 2,500 | 3,000 | 3,500 | 1,000 | 1,500 | 1,500 | 22,000 |
| Gross Profit on sales | 7,600 | 11,400 | 15,200 | 11,400 | 7,600 | 15,200 | 19,000 | 22,800 | 26,600 | 7,600 | 11,400 | 11,400 | 167,200 |
| Other revenues | 2,000 | 2,000 | 2,000 | 2,000 | 2,000 | 2,000 | 2,000 | 2,000 | 2,000 | 2,000 | 2,000 | 2,000 | 24,000 |
| Gross Profit | 9,600 | 13,400 | 17,200 | 13,400 | 9,600 | 17,200 | 21,000 | 24,800 | 28,600 | 9,600 | 13,400 | 13,400 | 191,200 |
| | | | | | | | | | | | | | 0 |
| Operating Expenses | | | | | | | | | | | | | 0 |
| Payroll | 7,500 | 7,500 | 7,500 | 7,500 | 7,500 | 7,500 | 7,500 | 7,500 | 7,500 | 7,500 | 6,000 | 6,000 | 87,000 |
| Benefits -13% payroll | 975 | 975 | 975 | 975 | 975 | 975 | 975 | 975 | 975 | 975 | 780 | 780 | 11,310 |
| Rent | 2,300 | 2,300 | 2,300 | 2,300 | 2,300 | 2,300 | 2,300 | 2,300 | 2,300 | 2,300 | 2,300 | 2,300 | 27,600 |
| Maintenance and Repairs | 250 | 250 | 250 | 250 | 250 | 250 | 250 | 250 | 250 | 250 | 250 | 250 | 3,000 |
| Advertising and Promotion | 2,000 | 2,000 | 4,000 | 2,000 | 2,000 | 4,000 | 6,000 | 6,000 | 6,000 | 2,000 | 2,000 | 2,000 | 40,000 |
| Legal and Accounting | 500 | 500 | 500 | 500 | 500 | 500 | 500 | 500 | 500 | 500 | 500 | 500 | 6,000 |
| Travel | 700 | 1,000 | 2,500 | 700 | 700 | 1,200 | 700 | 2,500 | 2,500 | 700 | 700 | 700 | 14,600 |
| Depreciation | 1,000 | 1,000 | 1,000 | 1,000 | 1,000 | 1,000 | 1,000 | 1,000 | 1,000 | 1,000 | 1,000 | 1,000 | 12,000 |
| Interest - 1.2% End N/P | 348 | 336 | 324 | 312 | 300 | 288 | 276 | 264 | 252 | 240 | 228 | 216 | 3,384 |
| Insurance | 700 | 700 | 700 | 700 | 700 | 700 | 700 | 700 | 700 | 700 | 700 | 700 | 8,400 |
| Utilities | 500 | 500 | 500 | 500 | 500 | 700 | 1,000 | 1,000 | 1,000 | 500 | 500 | 500 | 7,700 |
| Total Operating Expenses | 16,773 | 17,061 | 20,549 | 16,737 | 16,725 | 19,413 | 21,201 | 22,989 | 22,977 | 16,665 | 14,958 | 14,946 | 220,994 |
| Net Profit before taxes | -7,173 | -3,661 | -3,349 | -3,337 | -7,125 | -2,213 | -201 | 1,811 | 5,623 | -7,065 | -1,558 | -1,546 | -29,794 |
| Estimated Tax - 30% Net Profit | -2,152 | -1,098 | -1,005 | -1,001 | -2,137 | -664 | -60 | 543 | 1,687 | -2,119 | -467 | -464 | -8,938 |
| Net Profit | -5,021 | -2,563 | -2,344 | -2,336 | -4,987 | -1,549 | -141 | 1,268 | 3,936 | -4,945 | -1,091 | -1,082 | -20,856 |
| | | | | | | | | | | | | | |
| Beginning A/P | 40,000 | 38,522 | 41,686 | 38,743 | 32,523 | 39,524 | 47,026 | 52,807 | 58,532 | 37,869 | 33,815 | 35,317 | |
| Net Purchases | 16,500 | 22,000 | 16,500 | 11,000 | 22,000 | 27,500 | 33,000 | 38,500 | 11,000 | 16,500 | 16,500 | 27,500 | |
| <disc taken> 1% payments | 178 | 186 | 192 | 170 | 148 | 193 | 269 | 324 | 313 | 203 | 148 | 187 | |

| | C1 | C2 | C3 | C4 | C5 | C6 | C7 | C8 | C9 | C10 | C11 | C12 | Total |
|---|---|---|---|---|---|---|---|---|---|---|---|---|---|
| **<payments>** | | | | | | | | | | | | | |
| 20% current purchases | 3,300 | 4,400 | 3,300 | 2,200 | 4,400 | 5,500 | 6,600 | 7,700 | 2,200 | 3,300 | 3,300 | 5,500 | |
| 50% month - 1 | 10,000 | 8,250 | 11,000 | 8,250 | 5,500 | 11,000 | 13,750 | 16,500 | 19,250 | 5,500 | 8,250 | 8,250 | |
| 30% month - 2 | 4,500 | 6,000 | 4,950 | 6,600 | 4,950 | 3,300 | 6,600 | 8,250 | 9,900 | 11,550 | 3,300 | 4,950 | |
| <total payments> | 17,800 | 18,650 | 19,250 | 17,050 | 14,850 | 19,800 | 26,950 | 32,450 | 31,350 | 20,350 | 14,850 | 18,700 | |
| Ending A/P | 38,522 | 41,686 | 38,743 | 32,523 | 39,524 | 47,026 | 52,807 | 58,532 | 37,869 | 33,815 | 35,317 | 43,930 | |
| Increase in A/P | -1,478 | 3,164 | -2,943 | -6,220 | 7,002 | 7,502 | 5,781 | 5,726 | -20,663 | -4,054 | 1,502 | 8,613 | |
| | | | | | | | | | | | | | |
| Beginning Inventory | 70,000 | 75,500 | 81,000 | 75,500 | 70,000 | 81,000 | 86,500 | 92,000 | 97,500 | 70,000 | 75,500 | 75,500 | |
| <Sales X 55%> | 11,000 | 16,500 | 22,000 | 16,500 | 11,000 | 22,000 | 27,500 | 33,000 | 38,500 | 11,000 | 16,500 | 16,500 | |
| Sales month +1 X 55% | 16,500 | 22,000 | 16,500 | 11,000 | 22,000 | 27,500 | 33,000 | 38,500 | 11,000 | 16,500 | 16,500 | 27,500 | |
| Ending Inventory | 75,500 | 81,000 | 75,500 | 70,000 | 81,000 | 86,500 | 92,000 | 97,500 | 70,000 | 75,500 | 75,500 | 86,500 | |
| Change in Inventory | 5,500 | 5,500 | -5,500 | -5,500 | 11,000 | 5,500 | 5,500 | 5,500 | -27,500 | 5,500 | 0 | 11,000 | |
| Net Purchases | 16,500 | 22,000 | 16,500 | 11,000 | 22,000 | 27,500 | 33,000 | 38,500 | 11,000 | 16,500 | 16,500 | 27,500 | |
| | | | | | | | | | | | | | |
| Beginning N/P | 30,000 | 29,000 | 28,000 | 27,000 | 26,000 | 25,000 | 24,000 | 23,000 | 22,000 | 21,000 | 20,000 | 19,000 | |
| <Repayments> | 1,000 | 1,000 | 1,000 | 1,000 | 1,000 | 1,000 | 1,000 | 1,000 | 1,000 | 1,000 | 1,000 | 1,000 | |
| Loan Proceeds | 0 | 0 | 0 | 0 | 0 | 0 | 0 | 0 | 0 | 0 | 0 | 0 | |
| Ending N/P | 29,000 | 28,000 | 27,000 | 26,000 | 25,000 | 24,000 | 23,000 | 22,000 | 21,000 | 20,000 | 19,000 | 18,000 | |
| In-de>crease in N/P | -1,000 | -1,000 | -1,000 | -1,000 | -1,000 | -1,000 | -1,000 | -1,000 | -1,000 | -1,000 | -1,000 | -1,000 | |
| | | | | | | | | | | | | | |
| Beginning Cash | 10,000 | 3,501 | 4,102 | -1,185 | -9,741 | -7,727 | -1,775 | 3,865 | 10,858 | -5,869 | -14,868 | ##### | |
| Net Income | -5,021 | -2,563 | -2,344 | -2,336 | -4,987 | -1,549 | -141 | 1,268 | 3,936 | -4,945 | -1,091 | -1,082 | -20,856 |
| Depreciation | 1,000 | 1,000 | 1,000 | 1,000 | 1,000 | 1,000 | 1,000 | 1,000 | 1,000 | 1,000 | 1,000 | 1,000 | 12,000 |
| In-de>crease in A/P | -1,478 | 3,164 | -2,943 | -6,220 | 7,002 | 7,502 | 5,781 | 5,726 | -20,663 | -4,054 | 1,502 | 8,613 | 3,930 |
| In-de>crease in Loans | -1,000 | -1,000 | -1,000 | -1,000 | -1,000 | -1,000 | -1,000 | -1,000 | -1,000 | -1,000 | -1,000 | -1,000 | -12,000 |
| Ending Cash | 3,501 | 4,102 | -1,185 | -9,741 | -7,727 | -1,775 | 3,865 | 10,858 | -5,869 | -14,868 | -14,457 | -6,926 | |

| | JAN | FEB | MAR | APR | MAY | JUN | JUL | AUG | SEP | OCT | NOV | DEC | TOTAL |
|---|---|---|---|---|---|---|---|---|---|---|---|---|---|
| Gross sales | 30,000 | 40,000 | 50,000 | 40,000 | 30,000 | 50,000 | 60,000 | 70,000 | 80,000 | 30,000 | 40,000 | 40,000 | 560,000 |
| <Discounts and Returns - 2%> | 600 | 800 | 1,000 | 800 | 600 | 1,000 | 1,200 | 1,400 | 1,600 | 600 | 800 | 800 | 11,200 |
| Net Sales | 29,400 | 39,200 | 49,000 | 39,200 | 29,400 | 49,000 | 58,800 | 68,600 | 78,400 | 29,400 | 39,200 | 39,200 | 548,800 |
| <Cost of goods - 60%> | 18,000 | 24,000 | 30,000 | 24,000 | 18,000 | 30,000 | 36,000 | 42,000 | 48,000 | 18,000 | 24,000 | 24,000 | 336,000 |
| <Commissions - 5%> | 1,500 | 2,000 | 2,500 | 2,000 | 1,500 | 2,500 | 3,000 | 3,500 | 4,000 | 1,500 | 2,000 | 2,000 | 28,000 |
| Gross Profit on sales | 9,900 | 13,200 | 16,500 | 13,200 | 9,900 | 16,500 | 19,800 | 23,100 | 26,400 | 9,900 | 13,200 | 13,200 | 184,800 |
| Other revenues | 2,000 | 2,000 | 2,000 | 2,000 | 2,000 | 2,000 | 2,000 | 2,000 | 2,000 | 2,000 | 2,000 | 2,000 | 24,000 |
| Gross Profit | 11,900 | 15,200 | 18,500 | 15,200 | 11,900 | 18,500 | 21,800 | 25,100 | 28,400 | 11,900 | 15,200 | 15,200 | 208,800 |
| | | | | | | | | | | | | | 0 |
| | | | | | | | | | | | | | 0 |
| Operating Expenses | | | | | | | | | | | | | |
| Payroll | 7,500 | 7,500 | 7,500 | 7,500 | 7,500 | 7,500 | 7,500 | 7,500 | 7,500 | 7,500 | 7,500 | 7,500 | 87,000 |
| Benefits - 13% payroll | 975 | 975 | 975 | 975 | 975 | 975 | 975 | 975 | 975 | 975 | 780 | 780 | 11,310 |
| Rent | 2,300 | 2,300 | 2,300 | 2,300 | 2,300 | 2,300 | 2,300 | 2,300 | 2,300 | 2,300 | 2,300 | 2,300 | 27,600 |
| Maintenance and Repairs | 250 | 250 | 250 | 250 | 250 | 250 | 250 | 250 | 250 | 250 | 250 | 250 | 3,000 |
| Advertising and Promotion | 2,000 | 2,000 | 4,000 | 2,000 | 2,000 | 4,000 | 6,000 | 6,000 | 6,000 | 2,000 | 2,000 | 2,000 | 40,000 |
| Legal and Accounting | 500 | 500 | 500 | 500 | 500 | 500 | 500 | 500 | 500 | 500 | 500 | 500 | 6,000 |
| Travel | 700 | 1,000 | 2,500 | 1,000 | 1,000 | 1,200 | 700 | 2,500 | 2,500 | 700 | 700 | 700 | 14,600 |
| Depreciation | 1,000 | 1,000 | 1,000 | 1,000 | 1,000 | 1,000 | 1,000 | 1,000 | 1,000 | 1,000 | 1,000 | 1,000 | 12,000 |
| Interest - 1.2% End N/P | 348 | 336 | 324 | 312 | 300 | 288 | 276 | 264 | 252 | 240 | 228 | 216 | 3,384 |
| Insurance | 700 | 700 | 700 | 700 | 700 | 700 | 700 | 700 | 700 | 700 | 700 | 700 | 8,400 |
| Utilities | 500 | 500 | 500 | 500 | 500 | 700 | 1,000 | 1,000 | 1,000 | 500 | 500 | 500 | 7,700 |
| Total Operating Expenses | 16,773 | 17,061 | 20,549 | 16,737 | 16,725 | 19,413 | 21,201 | 22,989 | 22,977 | 16,665 | 14,958 | 14,946 | 220,994 |
| Net Profit before taxes | -4,873 | -1,861 | -2,049 | -1,537 | -4,825 | -913 | 599 | 2,111 | 5,423 | -4,765 | 242 | 254 | -12,194 |
| Estimated Tax - 30% Net Profit | -1,462 | -558 | -615 | -461 | -1,447 | -274 | 180 | 633 | 1,627 | -1,429 | 73 | 76 | -3,658 |
| Net Profit | -3,411 | -1,303 | -1,434 | -1,076 | -3,377 | -639 | 419 | 1,478 | 3,796 | -3,335 | 169 | 178 | -8,536 |
| | | | | | | | | | | | | | |
| Beginning A/P | 40,000 | 42,911 | 47,686 | 44,689 | 38,413 | 45,360 | 52,807 | 58,532 | 64,203 | 43,484 | 39,376 | 40,822 | |
| Net Purchases | 22,000 | 27,500 | 22,000 | 16,500 | 27,500 | 33,000 | 38,500 | 44,000 | 16,500 | 22,000 | 22,000 | 27,500 | |
| <disc taken> - 1% payments | 189 | 225 | 247 | 225 | 203 | 253 | 324 | 379 | 368 | 258 | 203 | 231 | |
| <payments> | | | | | | | | | | | | | |
| 20% current purchases | 4,400 | 5,500 | 4,400 | 3,300 | 5,500 | 6,600 | 7,700 | 8,800 | 3,300 | 4,400 | 4,400 | 5,500 | |
| 50% month - 1 | 10,000 | 11,000 | 13,750 | 11,000 | 8,250 | 13,750 | 16,500 | 19,250 | 22,000 | 8,250 | 11,000 | 11,000 | |
| 30% month - 2 | 4,500 | 6,000 | 6,600 | 8,250 | 6,600 | 4,950 | 8,250 | 9,900 | 11,550 | 13,200 | 4,950 | 6,600 | |

| | | | | | | | | | | | | | Total |
|---|---|---|---|---|---|---|---|---|---|---|---|---|---|
| <total payments> | 18,900 | 22,500 | 24,750 | 22,550 | 20,350 | 25,300 | 32,450 | 37,950 | 36,850 | 25,850 | 20,350 | 23,100 | |
| Ending A/P | 42,911 | 47,686 | 44,689 | 38,413 | 45,360 | 52,807 | 58,532 | 64,203 | 43,484 | 39,376 | 40,822 | 44,991 | |
| Increase in A/P | 2,911 | 4,775 | -2,997 | -6,275 | 6,947 | 7,447 | 5,726 | 5,671 | -20,718 | -4,108 | 1,447 | 4,169 | |
| | | | | | | | | | | | | | |
| Beginning Inventory | 70,000 | 75,500 | 81,000 | 75,500 | 70,000 | 81,000 | 86,500 | 92,000 | 97,500 | 70,000 | 75,500 | 75,500 | |
| <Sales X 55%> | 16,500 | 22,000 | 27,500 | 22,000 | 16,500 | 27,500 | 33,000 | 38,500 | 44,000 | 16,500 | 22,000 | 22,000 | |
| Sales month +1 X 55% | 22,000 | 27,500 | 22,000 | 16,500 | 27,500 | 33,000 | 38,500 | 44,000 | 16,500 | 22,000 | 22,000 | 27,500 | |
| Ending Inventory | 75,500 | 81,000 | 75,500 | 70,000 | 81,000 | 86,50C | 92,000 | 97,500 | 70,000 | 75,500 | 75,500 | 81,000 | |
| Change in Inventory | 5,500 | 5,500 | -5,500 | -5,500 | 11,000 | 5,500 | 5,500 | 5,500 | -27,500 | 5,500 | 0 | 5,500 | |
| Net Purchases | 22,000 | 27,500 | 22,000 | 16,500 | 27,500 | 33,000 | 38,500 | 44,000 | 16,500 | 22,000 | 22,000 | 27,500 | |
| | | | | | | | | | | | | | |
| Beginning N/P | 30,000 | 29,000 | 28,000 | 27,000 | 26,000 | 25,000 | 24,000 | 23,000 | 22,000 | 21,000 | 20,000 | 19,000 | |
| <Repayments> | 1,000 | 1,000 | 1,000 | 1,000 | 1,000 | 1,000 | 1,000 | 1,000 | 1,000 | 1,000 | 1,000 | 1,000 | |
| Loan Proceeds | 0 | 0 | 0 | 0 | 0 | 0 | 0 | 0 | 0 | 0 | 0 | 0 | |
| Ending N/P | 29,000 | 28,000 | 27,000 | 26,000 | 25,000 | 24,000 | 23,000 | 22,000 | 21,000 | 20,000 | 19,000 | 18,000 | |
| In<de>crease in N/P | -1,000 | -1,000 | -1,000 | -1,000 | -1,000 | -1,000 | -1,000 | -1,000 | -1,000 | -1,000 | -1,000 | -1,000 | |
| | | | | | | | | | | | | | |
| Beginning Cash | 10,000 | 9,500 | 12,972 | 8,540 | 1,189 | 4,758 | 11,566 | 17,711 | 24,859 | 7,937 | 493 | 2,108 | |
| Net Income | -3,411 | -1,303 | -1,434 | -1,076 | -3,377 | -659 | 419 | 1,478 | 3,796 | -3,335 | 169 | 178 | -8,536 |
| Depreciation | 1,000 | 1,000 | 1,000 | 1,000 | 1,000 | 1,000 | 1,000 | 1,000 | 1,000 | 1,000 | 1,000 | 1,000 | 12,000 |
| In<de>crease in A/P | 2,911 | 4,775 | -2,997 | -6,275 | 6,947 | 7,447 | 5,726 | 5,671 | -20,718 | -4,108 | 1,447 | 4,169 | 4,991 |
| In<de>crease in Loans | -1,000 | -1,000 | -1,000 | -1,000 | -1,000 | -1,000 | -1,000 | -1,000 | -1,000 | -1,000 | -1,000 | -1,000 | -12,000 |
| Ending Cash | 9,500 | 12,972 | 8,540 | 1,189 | 4,758 | 11,566 | 17,711 | 24,859 | 7,937 | 493 | 2,108 | 6,455 | |

| | JAN | FEB | MAR | APR | MAY | JUN | JUL | AUG | SEP | OCT | NOV | DEC | TOTAL |
|---|---|---|---|---|---|---|---|---|---|---|---|---|---|
| Gross sales | 30,000 | 40,000 | 50,000 | 40,000 | 30,000 | 50,000 | 60,000 | 70,000 | 80,000 | 30,000 | 40,000 | 40,000 | 560,000 |
| <Discounts and Returns - 2%> | 600 | 800 | 1,000 | 800 | 600 | 1,000 | 1,200 | 1,400 | 1,600 | 600 | 800 | 800 | 11,200 |
| Net Sales | 29,400 | 39,200 | 49,000 | 39,200 | 29,400 | 49,000 | 58,800 | 68,600 | 78,400 | 29,400 | 39,200 | 39,200 | 548,800 |
| <Cost of goods - 55%> | 16,500 | 22,000 | 27,500 | 22,000 | 16,500 | 27,500 | 33,000 | 38,500 | 44,000 | 16,500 | 22,000 | 22,000 | 308,000 |
| <Commissions - 5%> | 1,500 | 2,000 | 2,500 | 2,000 | 1,500 | 2,500 | 3,000 | 3,500 | 4,000 | 1,500 | 2,000 | 2,000 | 28,000 |
| Gross Profit on sales | 11,400 | 15,200 | 19,000 | 15,200 | 11,400 | 19,000 | 22,800 | 26,600 | 30,400 | 11,400 | 15,200 | 15,200 | 212,800 |
| Other revenues | 2,000 | 2,000 | 2,000 | 2,000 | 2,000 | 2,000 | 2,000 | 2,000 | 2,000 | 2,000 | 2,000 | 2,000 | 24,000 |
| Gross Profit | 13,400 | 17,200 | 21,000 | 17,200 | 13,400 | 21,000 | 24,800 | 28,600 | 32,400 | 13,400 | 17,200 | 17,200 | 236,800 |
| | | | | | | | | | | | | | 0 |
| Operating Expenses | | | | | | | | | | | | | 0 |
| Payroll | 7,500 | 7,500 | 7,500 | 7,500 | 7,500 | 7,500 | 7,500 | 7,500 | 7,500 | 7,500 | 6,000 | 6,000 | 87,000 |
| Benefits -13% payroll | 975 | 975 | 975 | 975 | 975 | 975 | 975 | 975 | 975 | 975 | 780 | 780 | 11,310 |
| Rent | 2,300 | 2,300 | 2,300 | 2,300 | 2,300 | 2,300 | 2,300 | 2,300 | 2,300 | 2,300 | 2,300 | 2,300 | 27,600 |
| Maintenance and Repairs | 250 | 250 | 250 | 250 | 250 | 250 | 250 | 250 | 250 | 250 | 250 | 250 | 3,000 |
| Advertising and Promotion | 2,000 | 2,000 | 4,000 | 2,000 | 2,000 | 4,000 | 6,000 | 6,000 | 6,000 | 2,000 | 2,000 | 2,000 | 40,000 |
| Legal and Accounting | 500 | 500 | 500 | 500 | 500 | 500 | 500 | 500 | 500 | 500 | 500 | 500 | 6,000 |
| Travel | 700 | 1,000 | 2,500 | 700 | 700 | 1,200 | 700 | 2,500 | 2,500 | 700 | 700 | 700 | 14,600 |
| Depreciation | 1,000 | 1,000 | 1,000 | 1,000 | 1,000 | 1,000 | 1,000 | 1,000 | 1,000 | 1,000 | 1,000 | 1,000 | 12,000 |
| Interest - 1.2% End N/P | 330 | 300 | 270 | 240 | 210 | 180 | 150 | 120 | 90 | 60 | 30 | 0 | 1,980 |
| Insurance | 700 | 700 | 700 | 700 | 700 | 700 | 700 | 700 | 700 | 700 | 700 | 700 | 8,400 |
| Utilities | 500 | 500 | 500 | 500 | 500 | 700 | 1,000 | 1,000 | 1,000 | 500 | 500 | 500 | 7,700 |
| Total Operating Expenses | 16,755 | 17,025 | 20,495 | 16,665 | 16,635 | 19,305 | 21,075 | 22,845 | 22,815 | 16,485 | 14,760 | 14,730 | 219,590 |
| Net Profit before taxes | -3,355 | 175 | 505 | 535 | -3,235 | 1,695 | 3,725 | 5,755 | 9,585 | -3,085 | 2,440 | 2,470 | 17,210 |
| Estimated Tax - 30% Net Profit | -1,006 | 53 | 152 | 161 | -970 | 509 | 1,118 | 1,727 | 2,876 | -925 | 732 | 741 | 5,163 |
| Net Profit | -2,348 | 123 | 354 | 375 | -2,264 | 1,187 | 2,608 | 4,029 | 6,710 | -2,159 | 1,708 | 1,729 | 12,047 |
| | | | | | | | | | | | | | |
| Beginning A/P | 40,000 | 42,911 | 47,686 | 44,689 | 38,413 | 45,360 | 52,807 | 58,532 | 64,203 | 43,484 | 39,376 | 40,822 | |
| Net Purchases | 22,000 | 27,500 | 22,000 | 16,500 | 27,500 | 33,000 | 38,500 | 44,000 | 16,500 | 22,000 | 22,000 | 27,500 | |
| <disc taken> - 1% payments | 189 | 225 | 247 | 225 | 203 | 253 | 324 | 379 | 368 | 258 | 203 | 231 | |
| <payments> | | | | | | | | | | | | | |
| 20% current purchases | 4,400 | 5,500 | 4,400 | 3,300 | 5,500 | 6,600 | 7,700 | 8,800 | 3,300 | 4,400 | 4,400 | 5,500 | |
| 50% month - 1 | 10,000 | 11,000 | 13,750 | 11,000 | 8,250 | 13,750 | 16,500 | 19,250 | 22,000 | 8,250 | 11,000 | 11,000 | |

| | 1 | 2 | 3 | 4 | 5 | 6 | 7 | 8 | 9 | 10 | 11 | 12 | Total |
|---|---|---|---|---|---|---|---|---|---|---|---|---|---|
| 30% month - 2 | 4,500 | 6,000 | 6,600 | 8,250 | 6,600 | 4,950 | 8,250 | 9,900 | 11,550 | 13,200 | 4,950 | 6,600 | |
| <total payments> | 18,900 | 22,500 | 24,750 | 22,550 | 20,350 | 25,300 | 32,450 | 37,950 | 36,850 | 25,850 | 20,350 | 23,100 | |
| Ending A/P | 42,911 | 47,686 | 44,689 | 38,413 | 45,360 | 52,807 | 58,532 | 64,203 | 43,484 | 39,376 | 40,822 | 44,991 | |
| Increase in A/P | 2,911 | 4,775 | -2,997 | -6,275 | 6,947 | 7,447 | 5,726 | 5,671 | -20,718 | -4,108 | 1,447 | 4,169 | |
| | | | | | | | | | | | | | |
| Beginning Inventory | 70,000 | 75,500 | 81,000 | 75,500 | 70,000 | 81,000 | 86,500 | 92,000 | 97,500 | 70,000 | 75,500 | 75,500 | |
| <Sales X 55%> | 16,500 | 22,000 | 27,500 | 22,000 | 16,500 | 27,500 | 33,000 | 38,500 | 44,000 | 16,500 | 22,000 | 22,000 | |
| Sales month +1 X 55% | 22,000 | 27,500 | 22,000 | 16,500 | 27,500 | 33,000 | 38,500 | 44,000 | 16,500 | 22,000 | 22,000 | 27,500 | |
| Ending Inventory | 75,500 | 81,000 | 75,500 | 70,000 | 81,000 | 86,500 | 92,000 | 97,500 | 70,000 | 75,500 | 75,500 | 81,000 | |
| Change in Inventory | 5,500 | 5,500 | -5,500 | -5,500 | 11,000 | 5,500 | 5,500 | 5,500 | -27,500 | 5,500 | 0 | 5,500 | |
| Net Purchases | 22,000 | 27,500 | 22,000 | 16,500 | 27,500 | 33,000 | 38,500 | 44,000 | 16,500 | 22,000 | 22,000 | 27,500 | |
| | | | | | | | | | | | | | |
| Beginning N/P | 30,000 | 27,500 | 25,000 | 22,500 | 20,000 | 17,500 | 15,000 | 12,500 | 10,000 | 7,500 | 5,000 | 2,500 | |
| <Repayments> | 2,500 | 2,500 | 2,500 | 2,500 | 2,500 | 2,500 | 2,500 | 2,500 | 2,500 | 2,500 | 2,500 | 2,500 | |
| Loan Proceeds | 0 | 0 | 0 | 0 | 0 | 0 | 0 | 0 | 0 | 0 | 0 | 0 | |
| Ending N/P | 27,500 | 25,000 | 22,500 | 20,000 | 17,500 | 15,000 | 12,500 | 10,000 | 7,500 | 5,000 | 2,500 | 0 | |
| In<de>-crease in N/P | -2,500 | -2,500 | -2,500 | -2,500 | -2,500 | -2,500 | -2,500 | -2,500 | -2,500 | -2,500 | -2,500 | -2,500 | |
| | | | | | | | | | | | | | |
| Beginning Cash | 10,000 | 9,063 | 12,460 | 8,316 | 915 | 4,097 | 11,231 | 18,064 | 26,263 | 10,754 | 2,986 | 4,640 | |
| Net Income | -2,348 | 123 | 354 | 375 | -2,264 | 1,187 | 2,608 | 4,029 | 6,710 | -2,159 | 1,708 | 1,729 | 12,047 |
| Depreciation | 1,000 | 1,000 | 1,000 | 1,000 | 1,000 | 1,000 | 1,000 | 1,000 | 1,000 | 1,000 | 1,000 | 1,000 | 12,000 |
| In<de>-crease in A/P | 2,911 | 4,775 | -2,997 | -6,275 | 6,947 | 7,447 | 5,726 | 5,671 | -20,718 | -4,108 | 1,447 | 4,169 | 4,991 |
| In<de>-crease in Loans | -2,500 | -2,500 | -2,500 | -2,500 | -2,500 | -2,500 | -2,500 | -2,500 | -2,500 | -2,500 | -2,500 | -2,500 | -30,000 |
| Ending Cash | 9,063 | 12,460 | 8,316 | 915 | 4,097 | 11,231 | 18,064 | 26,263 | 10,754 | 2,986 | 4,640 | 9,038 | |

In the first example, we merely subtracted sales of $10,000 per month.

In the second, we increase the cost of sales to 60%. And in the third, we increased the loan pay-back to $2500 per month.

If your business is substantially more complicated than this example, and you do not feel as though you can use the above tutorial to create your own program, check with your CPA for the name of someone who can set up your program. It would also be a good idea to have your CPA look at your forecast to see if there are any mistakes in the formulations or assumptions.

## Interpretation

You have now produced a complete set of instruments through which you can plan various strategies for the rest of your business. Without these tools you'll fly blind into decisions that can destroy your shop as surely as a pilot would lose his aircraft if he were to operate without benefit of radar, flight plan, or gauges.

Through these various instruments you will know whether you can afford another piece of equipment, another employee, or an increase in your advertising budget. They provide an early warning system that will predict a temporary cash shortage caused by rapid growth or the launching of a new product line. By running through various scenarios you will be able to foresee the effects of a sales slump or loss of a credit line.

Another major use for these various financial reports is for comparison with actual results. At the end of each month or other period for which you have financial data, you can plug in the real numbers and see how well your forecasting worked. It is one thing to predict sales numbers and see how your estimates pan out, but the real test of your ability comes when you begin to see whether you are meeting your estimates of gross profit percentage, inventory turns, or days to collect receivables.

As you compare each month's figures, you will begin to hone your estimates for future months. By the sixth month or so, you should begin to see your predictions come close to the real world.

If not, it may be time to see your CPA or other professional to see why you are missing the boat. In fact, you may want to begin the entire process of setting up these spread sheets in your computer through your CPA. Then later, you can compare your results together. If your accountant is good at what he does, this time together could provide excellent insights into ways to better manage your business.

# APPENDIX

# BOOK LIST

1. *Think and Grow Rich*, Napoleon Hill
2. *How I Raised Myself From Failure to Success in Selling*, Frank Bettger
3. *The Power of Positive Thinking*, Norman Vincent Peale
4. *The Greatest Salesman in the World*, Og Mondigo
5. *Psycho-Cybernetics*, Maxwell Maltz
6. *How to Win Friends and Influence People*, Dale Carnegie
7. *How to Stop Worrying and Start Living*, Dale Carnegie
8. *Go For It*, Dr. Irene Kassorla
9. *Success Forces*, Joseph Sugarman
10. *Looking Out For #1*, Robert Ringer
11. *Megatrends*, John Naisbitt
12. *In Search of Excellence*, Thomas Peters & Robert Waterman
13. *Positioning*, Al Reis
14. *What They Don't Teach You at the Harvard Business School*, Mark H. McCormack
15. *Marketing Welfare*, Al Reis
16. *Wealth Without Risk*, Charles Givens
17. *Seeds of Greatness*, Denis Waitley

# HEN FRIDAY ISN'T PAYDAY

*Complete Guide to Starting, Running—and Surviving In—a Very Small Business*

**NDY W. KIRK**

**FEBRUARY**

**ISBN:**
0-446-39398-3

**PRICE:**
$12.99
(In Canada: $16.25)

**CATEGORY:**
Business
(CPDA/IPDA #77)

**PUBLISHING BACKGROUND:**
Warner original

**PAGES:**
352

**SPINE SIZE:**
13/16"

**PER CARTON:**
20

**TRIM SIZE:**
6×9

**AUTHOR'S HOME:**
Inglewood, CA

**RIGHTS:**
World English

om pipe dream to opening day and beyond,
much-needed guide tells readers how to start
operate their own very small business. It fo-
s on critical issues such as:

- Selling
- Marketing
- Vendor relations
- Collecting accounts
- Making payroll
- Surviving long enough to turn the project into
an asset

, it's one of the few books to help would-be
preneurs answer the tough question, "Do I
y want to do this?"

ddresses the crucial issue of not only how to
age a very small business, but how to *survive*
very small business.

pplies basic business rules of buying, sell-
hiring, financing, and promoting to small
ness.

■ Expert author has operated 14 different "very
small businesses," is president of AC International, a bicycle manufacturer and importer, and
has spoken to hundreds of groups on the subject of
small businesses. His book, *Principles of Bicycle
Retailing,* is considered the industry bible.

**"Offers page after page of useful advice for any-
one who wants to start a business. First, Kirk
helps you decide whether becoming an entrepre-
neur is right for you. Then he delivers a comprehensive guide to launching your business and
getting it through those crucial first couple
of years."** —Robert Casey, Editor,
*Your Company* magazine (1.1 million circ.)

**RANDY W. KIRK** is president of AC International and
CEO of Reliance Security, and had been involved
in small business for many years.

**ADVERTISING, PUBLICITY, PROMOTION:**
• Print advertising in *Small Business Opportunities, Business Ventures, Income Opportunities,*
and *Marketers Forum*

RIBUTOR: INFO NET PUBLISHNG • P.O. Box 3789 • San Clemente, CA 92674 • (714) 489-9292

# Bike Retailers:

## Here's how you can overcome the recession — by becoming pro-active and planning now to meet an economic downturn

Stay on top during tough times with…

BICYCLE RETAILERS GUIDE TO GETTING RICH IN THE RECESSION — a concise, detailed, easy-to-read — and implement — manual on how to survive — and prosper — in an economic downturn. Here's how…

By getting active to meet tough economic times, while other retailers are counting their pennies

By building a business with a pro-active attitude, while other retail businesses are sitting on the sidelines of defeat

By countering negative purchasing attitudes, and becoming aggressive marketers

Bicycle Retailers Guide to

# Getting Rich
# IN THE RECESSION

BY RANDY W. KIRK
Author of Principles of
Bicycle Retailing

Simple techniques for putting you on TOP during a downturn … or at any time.

---